Doing Business with

O m a n

FOR THE SECOND

CONSECUTIVE YEAR

GLOBAL FIN@NCE

AWARDS BANKMUSCAT

At BankMuscat we are proud of our achievements and awards. Achievements such as being voted the **'Best Bank in Oman 2002'**, by Global Finance magazine, New York. It's the second year in a row we have won this prestigious award. However, our greatest award is the satisfaction and delight of our customers.

Doing Business with

O m a n

Consultant Editor:
Philip Dew

Middle East Series Editor:
Anthony Shoult

With contributions from
Jonathan Wallace

Forewords by:
HE Maqbool Ali Sultan
Minister of Commerce & Industry
Sir Ivan Callan
HM Ambassador to Oman

in association with

Publisher's note

Every possible effort has been made to ensure that the information contained in this handbook is accurate at the time of going to press, and the publishers and authors cannot accept responsibility for any errors or omissions, however caused. No responsibility for loss or damage occasioned to any person acting, or refraining from action, as a result of the material in this publication can be accepted by the editor, the publisher or any of the authors.

The information provided by the contributors is solely to enable interested investors/business people to gain initial familiarity with the investment climate in Oman. Interested investors should undertake further investigation as they see fit before taking any investment decisions.

First published in 2002

Kogan Page Ltd
120 Pentonville Road
London N1 9JN
www.kogan-page.co.uk

© Kogan Page, ASA Consulting and Contributors 2002

British Library Cataloguing in Publication Data

A CIP record for this book is available from the British Library

ISBN 0 7494 3811 8

Typeset by JS Typesetting Ltd, Wellingborough, Northants
Printed and bound in Great Britain by Biddles Ltd, Guildford and King's Lynn
www.biddles.co.uk

AHLI UNITED BANK (AUB)

Ahli United Bank – the creation of a substantial international financial group from two successful banking institutions.

Ahli United Bank (AUB) does not merely constitute a larger version of United Bank of Kuwait (UBK) or Al-Ahli Commercial Bank (ACB), but a stronger and better institution altogether, with fresh challenges and greater growth potential than both predecessors. AUB now offers a more diversified product range, reaches a wider client base and has a broader geographical presence.

AUB is a fully-fledged commercial institution and investment bank providing wealth management, retail, corporate treasury, offshore and private banking services. It is geared towards growth through the development of a larger client base in the GCC states and of close partnership with customers, staff and product providers.

By continuing to focus on our clients' needs and relying on management's professional skills, we aim to achieve excellent performance for our shareholders on a year-by-year basis.

In addition to our stated intention of growing through mergers and acquisitions, the Bank's size and ability to move swiftly make it perfectly suited to a strategy of systematic growth, improved liquidity, greater market capitalization and enhanced quality of earnings.

It is intended to achieve this through fully utilizing AUB's larger geographical footprint and distribution network, and providing a high quality service to our customers through a wider portfolio of commercial and investment banking services. At the same time, streamlining our business will instill even greater financial discipline as we enter new markets, enhancing out technological capabilities and continuing to apply a very effective risk management strategy.

AUB is a commercially-driven organisation, committed to providing the highest levels of service to an increasing customer base, and to planned evolution through both organic growth and acquisitions. The Bank has brought together an experienced and talented professional team, dedicated to implementing management's vision through the application of market expertise and the latest technology.

Headquartered in Bahrain, the AUB Group operates within the regulatory framework of the Bahrain Monetary Agency (BMA), whilst its UK subsidiary is regulated by the Financial Services Authority (FSA) and investment Management Regulatory Organisation (IMRO).

The Bank employs some 500 staff in Bahrain, London, Kuwait, Dubai and the Channel Islands.

AUB's revenue business is organized into two divisions: Private Banking and Wealth Management and Commercial Banking and Treasury. The Risk, Finance and Strategic Development Group supports both these divisions and is responsible for the Group's expansion through mergers and acquisitions. The Regulatory and Support Group is responsible for internal and external compliance, and corporate governance issues.

Private banking is a key strategic element in AUB's expansion plans. This division includes all the non capital-intensive sectors of the business, offering customers an integrated wealth management service based on performance and a balanced product mix. Private banking combines discreet, personal care with expert financial support, ensuring that each client enjoys services catering to their individual scenario.

AUB private banking offers a comprehensive product portfolio including standard banking, investments and finance services, tax, inheritance and trust advice, along with wealth protection, structured lending and foreign exchange services. We also offer a wide range of traditional funds and alternative investment vehicles. Continuing improvements in methodology and concerted efforts in each Gulf market keep AUB's products at the forefront of investment solutions. AUB provides an innovative range of Asset Management products that reflect the Bank's customer focus. When looking to introduce investment management services to its Middle East operations, AUB established a joint venture with Mellon Global Investments. The new entity, Mellon Ahli Asset Management Ltd offers a wide range of services, including equity and debt management, complemented by total return hedge funds and capital protected structures. Crucially, the new structure allows AUB to focus its attention on client relationships whilst continually enhancing the available product portfolio.

Continued product innovation and greater access to customers in the Gulf has sustained steady progress in Islamic Banking area. AUB's range of Sharia'a based services provides a complementary option to the Bank's conventional product portfolio. Consistency in both quality and breadth of service means that GCC customers now have access to standard and sophisticated international banking and fund management services through their existing network. AUB also offers Morabaha services to corporations, providing money market type facilities in a Sharia'a compatible structure involving short-term trade financing with deferred settlement.

By recently initiating a new joint venture with Henderson Global Investors, a specialist in international real estate fund management, AUB is able to introduce more of its clients to the lucrative European markets. The result is a higher level of product quality which, supported by AUB's global resources and substantial technical expertise, makes for one of the most innovative property investment services available.

The Bank's traditional role as a key financial link was further supplemented by improved access to more Middle East markets for European exporters and we now enjoy a significant further commercial advantage in the ability to offer a service that is individually tailored as well as highly competitive.

For many years UBK has acted as a key financial link for European exporters seeking access to Middle Eastern markets, while AUB Bahrain has worked with clients in the Gulf region, including major private companies, financial institutions and the government. These two perspectives mean AUB can now identify greater opportunities in more markets – a trend that evolves as the Bank continues to build new corporate relationship in manufacturing, construction, trade and tourism throughout the region.

Structured Finance activities encompass three business lines. Acquisition finance – a dedicated team focuses on the origination of transactions derived from corporate merger and acquisitions activity. Collateralised obligations – in the high growth securitisation market the Bank can play significant role in the credit enhancement of special purpose structures. Bespoke project financing – primarily an advisory and structuring service for project sponsors.

The group's Treasury operations in Bahrain and London incorporates all the components essential to successful treasury management – innovative services, leading-edge technology, quality execution and resources. AUB's treasury management unit in Bahrain coordinates the group's proprietary trading and the provision on a wide range of products and services for a customer base including regional and local banks, corporates, institutions and high-net-worth investors.

These services include the quoting and trading of all major currencies including Gulf and regional currencies, deposits in all major currencies for all maturity periods, structured deposit accounts and a round-the clock foreign exchange service. We manage global interest rate risk on behalf of corporates and quote forward rate agreements, interest rate swaps, interest rate caps, collars and floors. In London treasury specializes in money market services and off-balance sheet instruments.

The Aviation Finance provides specialist finance to airlines and aircraft leasing companies around the world. Over the years the bank has earned a reputation for market knowledge, acumen and experience, and a significant client base has been developed in what is a highly specialized field. The Bank provides finance secured on commercial aircraft to operating lessors, either as a sole lender or as part of a syndicate. Our knowledge of this sector enabled the Bank to avoid any diminution in value in its investments after the September 11th events.

The Bank offers a competitive range of mortgage products, which it reviews continually, for property ventures in the office, retail and industrial sectors. The Bank is an experienced participant in international property finance and investment and has recently pioneered a series of commercial property securitisations in the UK. Joint venture financing proposals are considered, and the standard range of services includes investment loans secured on single assets or portfolios, mezzanine loans on the same basis and pre-let and speculative development finance.

The Bank provides a competitive and innovative range of mortgage products which it reviews continually to ensure consistent quality in an ever-changing marketplace. The Bank adheres to the highest lending standards and is a member of the Council of Mortgage Lenders. The Bank provides a fast and efficient service to individuals resident in the UK or overseas, trusts and corporate bodies.

Both UBK in London and AUB Bahrain offer a range of personal banking services which, over time, have anticipated and satisfied the needs of customers in each location. However, being committed to providing quality services means offering more than core products such as savings, current, deposit and fixed deposit accounts, or loans, credit cards and off-shore facilities. UBK offers first-class banking and investment services for Gulf nationals with business or personal interest in the UK and continental Europe. All activities are designed to support and complement the Bank's wealth management and investment services. With a network consisting of thirteen branches across the country, AUB Bahrain provides the full range of personal banking services.

In the first half of 2001, AUB announced two acquisitions which were powerful expressions of the Bank's strategy and significantly advance its regional aspirations.

In March 2001, AUB acquired a significant minority share in Bank of Kuwait and the Middle East (BKME) currently 18%.

In June 2001, AUB announced the merger of its wholly-owned subsidiary, Al-Ahli Commercial Bank, with Commercial Bank of Bahrain (CBB), formerly Grindlays Bahrain Bank Bsc. The combined entity has an approximate 21% share of the Bahrain onshore banking market and became fully operational on October 2001.

AUB has also established a joint venture with Mellon Global Investments, Mellon Ahli Asset Management Limited (Mellon Ahli), to offer investment management services in the Middle East, and a strategic alliance with United Bank of Kuwait and Henderson Global Investors to become the leading provider of real estate investment products in the Middle East.

These recent developments reflect AUB's determination to create a dynamic structure that offers its regional clients leading-edge financial opportunities, allied with the highest standards of customer service.

As a new bank in the Arab world with established roots, AUB is defining a fresh identity in the marketplace, creating organic growth and using mergers and acquisitions to bring consolidation to an oversaturated financial services sector.

A key component in fulfilling this strategy is the quality of our management team and the discipline with which we run our business. Our strengths are vision, focus and commitment.

The Group will realize significant operating efficiencies by leveraging technology platforms as we grow both domestically and internationally. These platforms will make it possible to expand sales of our products and enter new markets at a lower cost. At all times, we will remain customer focused and, looking forward, we will provide clients with an even greater range of solutions, becoming a more strategic part of their lives and decision making process.

At the core of the Bank's strategic planning are two key concepts. Firstly: complementarity – of customers, products, service, expertise and resources; and secondly: synergy – of people, markets and objectives. The Bank's faith in these attributes has proved to be well founded, and the future looks extremely promising as the potential of the demographically attractive Gulf customer base is matched by an enhanced product repertoire and distribution network. This will be further reinforced through the mobilization of AUB's marketing expertise to capitalize on acknowledged reputation for product, technological and corporate initiatives in identified business sectors based on the long standing involvement of its subsidiary bank in the region.

Contents

Part 6: Establishing Trading Links with Oman

Part 7: Marketing in Oman

Part 8: Labour Issues

Foreword

I am happy that Kogan Page, in association with the British Government's Trade Partners UK, is publishing *Doing Business with Oman*. I am pleased to learn that this is one of more than 70 publications published in the series, which has been enthusiastically received and appreciated by businessmen and investors all over the world.

This is an era that is witnessing revolutionary advances in information and communications technology (ICT). These have been triggered by, and in turn have profoundly impacted, the phenomenon of globalization in economic, social and cultural spheres. The speed with which, and the forms in which, information can be transmitted across national boundaries could not have been imagined a few decades ago. The process of opening up almost all economies of the world to flows of trade and capital can be immensely facilitated by the quick dissemination of reliable and authoritative information about the business opportunities available, the rules and regulations governing the establishment and operation of business entities in various countries, and the tax regimes applicable in them. In the competitive, globalized world of today, investment decisions as well as decisions on products, services and directions of trade are crucially dependent on the availability of up-to-date and reliable information and data.

I believe that *Doing Business with Oman* will provide a valuable insight into the very favourable environment for investment and trade opportunities that exists in the Sultanate and will also thus provide invaluable inputs for consideration by potential investors and business partners from various countries. Besides describing the essential features of the relevant laws, rules and regulations and potential economic opportunities available in Oman, this publication will hopefully provide a road map of practical utility during the process of setting up a business in Oman, selecting Omani partners and negotiating and managing joint ventures.

We have successfully completed our Fifth Five-Year Development Plan within our long-term 'Economic Vision 2020' and are currently implementing the Sixth Development Plan (2001–2005). With the accession of Oman to the World Trade Organization (WTO) already accomplished and the establishment of the AGCC (Arab Gulf Council Countries) Customs Union materializing by January 2003, the focus of

Vision 2020 will be on balanced and sustainable development of the private sector for achieving progressive diversification of the economy. As a part of this objective, the current Five-Year Development Plan places particular emphasis on implementing carefully formulated privatization programmes; natural-gas-based industrial projects; an investment programme for the development of tourism; information and communications technology; and human resources, which are crucial and critical for successful implementation of these programmes.

In pursuit of these objectives, the Omani government is determined to take, in a systematic manner, all necessary infrastructural, legal, procedural and promotional measures with a view to enhancing the productivity, efficiency and competitiveness of the economy.

In the above context, it is my hope and expectation that *Doing Business with Oman* will prove a valuable guide to prospective investors and businessmen who are attracted by the conducive, hospitable and business-friendly environment existing in Oman.

HE Maqbool Ali Sultan
Minister of Commerce and Industry, Sultanate of Oman

Foreword

The Sultanate of Oman and Britain are two maritime trading nations with a long history of commerce between them. Oman is a stable and secure nation lying outside the Gulf with excellent international credit ratings. Its people are educated and hospitable. The development of its physical, social, medical and educational infrastructure in recent decades has been remarkable and enviable. It is one of the best countries in which to live and doing business is becoming easier all the time. Oman is opening up its market to attract investment. It is determined to diversify its economy and build up its industrial base. It would welcome active participation and help, particularly in the form of joint ventures, which are the backbone of a long-term commercial relationship. The competitive tendering process is objective and fair and business practices are sound. The country's accession to the World Trade Organization (WTO) stimulated a programme of measures which are being implemented methodically and which further improve the Sultanate's attractiveness for business and investment.

I hope that *Doing Business with Oman* will ease the path to a potentially profitable and equally beautiful destination.

Sir Ivan Callan
British Ambassador, Sultanate of Oman

List of Contributors

Alaa Edin Mohamed Ahmed is responsible for Abu-Ghazaleh Intellectual Property, TMP Agents in Oman.

Mohsin bin Khamis Al-Balushi is under-secretary of tourism at the Omani Ministry of Commerce and Industry.

Hamed H Al Dhahab is director-general of industry at the Omani Ministry of Commerce and Industry.

Faisal AlHashar, an Omani national, has been corporate affairs and business development manager with Shell Oman Marketing Company since February 2001. He has a BSc in Marketing from the University of Missouri, United States, and held various posts in both the public and private sectors before joining Shell Oman.

Abdul Aziz Mohamed Al Hinai is acting general manager of Oman Development Bank (ODB).

Nasir bin Issa Al Ismaily is general manager of the Export Credit Guarantee Agency, Oman Development Bank.

Ahmed AlMarhoon is general manager of the Muscat Securities Market (MSM) in Oman.

Majid Al Toky is the senior Omani associate for Trowers & Hamlins' Oman office. Having acquired extensive experience as an in-house lawyer for Petroleum Development Oman, he now advises on concession agreements with the government of Oman, legal issues relating to oil and gas activities, and contracts and claims relating to such activities. Majid is also head of Trowers & Hamlins' litigation practice in Oman and appears before the courts representing both local and international clients on matters such as construction contracts, agencies, insurance, shipping, corporate and other commercial disputes.

Gordon Anderson is managing director of GC Anderson Consulting (Cyprus) and a consultant to Renaissance Education and Training Group in Oman. He has written numerous books and articles on performance appraisal, performance management, reward management and other aspects of human resource management and was named in the top 20 authorities on performance appraisal by the United Kingdom's Institute of Personnel Management. He has undertaken assignments for large, medium and small companies in regard to human resource management, many of which companies are household names internationally. He is a Fellow of the Chartered Institute of Personnel and Development, the Institute of Management and the Royal Society of Arts and Manufactures, all in the United Kingdom.

Sean Angle is Trowers & Hamlins' Oman office resident managing partner. He has been practising in Oman since 1990 and has extensive experience in corporate commercial and construction law, both contentious and non-contentious as well as major insurance litigation. He advises on capital markets as well as construction, EPC and BOO Scheme projects in the Middle East. Sean has also advised on international arbitrations as an expert in Omani law.

ASA Consulting is a UK-based independent marketing-focused consultancy specializing in the Middle East region. The firm provides a wide range of consultancy services across the industrial sectors, either directly or through affiliated organizations, to both international and local public- and private-sector agencies and organizations. The services provided include assistance to investors in specific areas such as market research and investigations for technical and industrial products and services and techno-economic feasibility studies to the highest standards.

Vipin Chandra is the country manager of Norwich Union Insurance (Gulf) Ltd in Oman.

Roger Clarke is Trowers & Hamlin's Middle East Regional Finance Partner. Roger has been primarily responsible for all project and project finance matters in the Oman office of Trowers & Hamlins and has extensive experience in the drafting and negotiating of complex project and project finance documents. In addition he has built a solid base in aircraft finance having written the Oman chapter of McBain and Hames *Aircraft Finance* and is included in Euromoney's *2000 Guide to the World's Leading Aviation Lawyers*.

Cluttons was formed in 1765 and is one of the leading firms of Chartered Surveyors and Property Consultants in the United Kingdom, with its head office in Berkeley Square in the heart of London. Since 1976, Cluttons has established a strong real-estate presence in the Middle East through its network of offices in the Arabian Gulf.

Ernst & Young, Oman. The firm commenced practising in the Sultanate in the mid-1950s, primarily to serve the needs of its oil and gas industry clients. A permanent office was opened in 1974. As local industry has grown and diversified throughout Oman, Ernst & Young has also expanded to meet clients' demands. In addition to having the largest tax practice, and being the largest provider of auditing services to the financial services industries in Oman, it is also one of the largest public accounting and management consulting firms operating in the Sultanate.

Ernst & Young is recognized as the leading tax practice in Oman. It currently advises the majority of the largest tax-paying companies in Oman and has developed longstanding professional relationships with all of the senior tax personnel at the Ministry of Finance. Its experience allows an opportunity to ascertain, at a very early stage, trends arising in Omani tax practices. As a result, Ernst & Young is able to provide proactive, timely advice to clients on changes likely to affect them.

Resident staff in Muscat number approximately 50, including three partners, the majority having been in Muscat or based in the firm's other offices in the Middle East for over five years.

Gregory R Greenwell took up his current position at Petroleum Development Oman in April 2000, having served for 11 years in various corporate-communication capacities within the Royal Dutch/Shell Group. Before joining Shell, he was a member of the board of editors of *Scientific American* magazine. He has a bachelor's degree from Rice University and a master's degree from the Massachusetts Institute of Technology.

Suhail Khan is manager, marketing research for SIMPA Marketing Research & Consultancy, based in Oman but with responsibility also for the company's Dubai operation. He has an MBA from the 105-year-old Osmania University in India and has worked in market research since 1993, firstly in India with leading research agencies and, since 1996, in the United Arab Emirates and Oman.

Val Kwaan is an English artist, writer and teacher who has lived in the Gulf States for almost 30 years, nine of them in Oman.

Michael Lowes is general manager of Cluttons, Muscat, having headed up the office since 1997. He is a qualified member of the Royal Institution of Chartered Surveyors with extensive property experience in the Middle East, Far East and United Kingdom.

Tausif Malik is the head of the newly formed Public Relations division of SIMPA. He has worked with major advertising agencies in India and the Middle East and on brands such as Sharp, Daewoo Color Monitors,

Veritas Software, Infosys and SCALA. He was the highest account biller in India for 1997–1998 in handling the then nascent IT industry. He has also handled well-known personalities in India. He has an MBA and an MCom, having majored in Marketing and Business Administration, respectively.

Radha Mukherjee is an Honours graduate in Statistics and has an MBA from IIM, Calcutta. She specializes in marketing and operations management and has varied work experience covering market research, product management and, for the last 18 years, advertising. She has worked for multinational agency networks such as Ogilvy's and JWT in India, and negotiated the tie-up between OHI and DDB for Oman in 1996, making DDB the first significant international agency presence in the country.

Norwich Union has been operating in Oman since 1971 through sponsors Zubair Travel & Service Bureau and transacts all classes of general insurance.

OHI DDB Advertising & Publicity Company is a leading advertising agency in Oman and the first that is truly a part of a global network. It handles the advertising for leading clients such as BankMuscat, Bahwan, Raha, Sanyo and KLM, among others.

Oman Capital Market Authority is the government body charged with overseeing the capital markets in Oman.

Omani Centre for Investment Promotion and Export Development is the government agency charged with assisting private-sector development in Oman through encouraging investment and supporting national companies in seeking markets outside the Sultanate for their locally manufactured products.

Nicholas Pattison has been managing director of Shell Oman Marketing Company since October 1998. On secondment from Shell International Petroleum Company, he has been with the Shell Group for 34 years. He has a bachelor's degree in Physics and a master's degree in Marketing. He has a wealth of experience in Shell companies in the distribution, retail and marketing functions and has been posted to various locations, including the United Kingdom, Philippines, India and United Arab Emirates. He is also a director of Oman Bitumen Company and JOSLOC in Riyadh, Saudi Arabia.

Philip Dew Consultancy Limited was founded in 1982 to support local and international principals in the comprehensive development of their businesses in the Middle East. The basic services provided include: identification, investigation and evaluation of market opportunities; market research and feasibility studies; identification of partners, principals and associates; development of marketing and business strategies; and on-the-ground support and assistance to market entrants, including the provision of background and cultural information. To date, assignments have been fulfilled for over 250 companies and individuals.

The business is owned and managed by **Philip Dew**, who has been in the Middle East for over 30 years, is an Arabic speaker and who acted as consultant on *Doing Business with the UAE*, *Doing Business with Bahrain* and *Doing Business with Iran* prior to being involved as consultant editor on this book and another on Qatar.

Philip Dew is based in Bahrain, from where he covers the whole Middle East.

Renaissance Holdings, Education and Training Group has been providing core vocational training and HSE training services in Oman since 1985. Programmes are delivered through training centres belonging to the following companies: National Training Institute (NTI) Muscat – HSE, Construction, Engineering, Fabrication, Auto Mechanics, Port Operations, Transport and Plant Operations; New Horizons Computer Learning Centres (NHCLC) Muscat – E-Learning and Information Technology; National Hospitality Institute (NHI) Muscat – Hospitality and Travel; Higher Institute of Administrative and Technical Sciences LLC (HIAT), Salalah Port Operations – Engineering, Construction, Manufacturing, Accounting, Commercial and Information Technology; Al Rakaib Training Institute, Muscat – Retailing, Commerce, Communications and Language.

Salalah Port Services Co is the company charged with the management and operation of the Salalah port.

SIMPA Marketing Research and Consultancy was Oman's first market research and public relations agency when established in 1996. The company is promoted by Western-educated Omani nationals with international experience, and has a highly educated, talented and experienced team of professionals with international exposure. The agency has worked for local and international companies, groups and brands. In 1999, an office was launched in Dubai to tap the UAE market, which houses the regional offices of many multinational companies. In 2001, the Public Relations division was formed as SIMPA-pr, which was the first PR agency in Oman. SIMPA is aligned with international marketing research and public relations agencies in the United States, Canada, India and Australia.

Sridhar Sridharan is the tax partner of Ernst & Young in Muscat. Sridhar has extensive experience in Oman taxation, having lived in Oman for 18 years. His areas of specialty include tax structuring entry advice, corporate tax planning, negotiating and concluding tax settlements in respect of controversial tax issues and successfully finalizing assessments for large multinational companies. Sridhar has also presented technical papers and lectured on tax-related issues in a number of seminars and conferences.

Andrew Rae is a partner in Trowers & Hamlins' Oman office. Andrew specializes and has extensive experience in project and general commercial work. He has extensive legal experience spanning nearly 20 years in the commercial and commercial litigation areas and is now regularly involved in advising foreign and local entities and public companies investing in Oman. He advises on tax and corporate structuring with specific emphasis on general commercial matters and tactical advice on corporate positioning.

Philip Stanton is managing partner of Ernst & Young, Muscat. Having worked for Ernst & Young in the region for over 15 years, including 10 years in Oman, Philip has significant experience in auditing, accounting and consultancy issues that are relevant to the area. His clients include government organizations, banks, oil and gas industry companies and a large number of multinational entities. Philip has advised several multinationals on investment strategies for entry into Oman, including listing on the Muscat Securities Market. He is closely associated with the Omani Centre for Investment Promotion and Export Development as a member of its Investment Working Group and is a member of the Accounting and Audit Committee advising the Capital Markets Authority.

Trowers & Hamlins are a pre-eminent London City law firm in the Middle East and are the current Chambers & Partners Middle East Law Firm of the Year. Trowers & Hamlins are made up of 64 partners and almost 400 staff and have branch offices in Oman, Abu Dhabi, Dubai, Bahrain and Cairo, with the largest and longest established of these being in Muscat, Oman (established in 1980). The firm has a significant presence in the Omani market and assists clients in the full range of commercial and business activities. It has clients from the public and private sectors, local and international, in many varied fields including banking and finance, energy, aviation, petrochemicals, manufacturing, engineering construction, agency and distribution and litigation.

Jeremy Williams OBE has spent more than 15 years in five Gulf locations: Sharjah, Dubai, Riyadh, Abu Dhabi and Bahrain. He was previously defence, naval, military and air attaché in the British Embassies in Abu Dhabi and Bahrain. His company, Handshaikh Ltd, offers bespoke induction seminars, advice and negotiation training that focus on the cross-cultural aspects of life and work in the Gulf.

His business book *Don't they know it's Friday?* (Motivate Publishing, Dubai, now in its 3rd reprint) addresses the cross-cultural aspects of Westerners' experiences with Gulf Arabs. Handshaikh Ltd: UK: Tel. +44 (0) 1962 771699, Fax. (0) 1962 771814, Dubai: Tel. (+971 4) 3517624, Fax. 3521033. Website: www.handshaikh.com; Email: mail:handshaikh.com.

Part 1

The Background

Geography and History

Philip Dew, Philip Dew Consultancy Limited, Bahrain

Geography

The Sultanate of Oman occupies 309,500 square kilometres (119,500 square miles) of the south-eastern extremity of the Arabian Peninsula. To the east and south-east, Oman has a coastline of 1,700 kilometres (1,506 miles) bordering three seas – the Arabian Gulf (in the far north along the Musandam Peninsula), the Gulf of Oman and the Arabian Sea; to the north is the United Arab Emirates; to the west are both the United Arab Emirates and Saudi Arabia; and to the south-west is the Republic of Yemen.

The Sultanate has a mixed terrain comprising mountains interspersed with fertile valleys; desert areas incapable of supporting human habitation and which border the Empty Quarter, the Rub' AlKhali, of Saudi Arabia; and a coastline fringed by fertile areas, particularly along the Batinah coast, which lies between the AlHajar mountains and the Gulf of Oman, and in the southern region of Dhofar in close proximity to Salalah, an area which benefits from the monsoon rains for several months of the year.

Oman's climate varies considerably from one region to another. Heat and humidity are major features of much of the coastal region in summer, although in the south this is tempered by the monsoon rains. In the interior, it is usually hot and dry except in the mountainous areas where night-time temperatures can fall considerably. During the winter, much of the country is pleasant and cool. The highest temperatures are reported to have been recorded in Sohar (on the Batinah coast) and the lowest on Jebel AlAkhdar in the interior, which also receives the highest level of rainfall. Mean temperatures in Muscat, the capital, vary between 20°C and 43°C, and the mean average rainfall in the city amounts to 100 millimetres.

The population of the country, which is predominantly of Arab origin but which also includes large numbers of Baluchis in addition to South

Asians and Africans, the latter mainly from Zanzibar and the neighbouring mainland, totals some 2.7 million. Population growth has historically been as high as 5 per cent per year, but more recent estimates suggest a figure below 4 per cent per year. Some 75 per cent of the population is Ibadi Muslim.

History

Little is known of Oman's earliest history, but traces of civilizations dating back some 7,000 years have been found and references to the land of Magan, which archaeologists believe may well be modern-day Oman, have been found on Sumerian tablets unearthed elsewhere in the region. Should Magan be Oman, the country was trading with cities such as Ur of the Chaldees some 5,000 years ago. In these early years, Oman was famous for its copper, which was mined at several sites around the country between 3,000 BC and 10th Century CE, and for its frankincense, which emanated from Dhofar in the south – both of which were shipped by land and sea to the major cities of the ancient world.

Islam came to Oman in 630 CE, thus making the country one of the first to absorb the new religion. Subsequently, a number of tribes in Oman embraced the Ibadi doctrine of Islam, which views the caliphate or leadership of Islam as neither hereditary nor the right of a single family, ultimately establishing an independent Imamate in Oman during the 9th Century CE. Over the ensuing years until modern times, and despite invasions from many directions including from the caliphate itself, the Iranians and the Mongols, Oman largely succeeded in remaining independent.

History records that the port of Sohar was probably the most important in the whole of Arabia in the 10th Century CE, with ships sailing from there to as far as China. Four hundred years later, when the Portuguese first sailed round southern Africa and into the Indian Ocean, they found that Oman maintained full control of the seas along its shores and that a number of Omani coastal towns enjoyed great prosperity, including Sohar, Qalhat and Muscat. The arrival of the Portuguese, however, changed the balance of power in the region as, over time, they established themselves by force in these ports.

Portuguese control lasted for over 100 years until members of the Ya'aruba Dynasty within Oman succeeded in overturning their rule throughout the eastern Indian Ocean littoral, including along the coast of East Africa in Mombasa and Zanzibar. Subsequently, the influence of the Ya'aruba declined and, in 1744, Ahmed bin Said, the Wali of Sohar, was elected Imam and set about re-unifying Oman, which had by that time also been subjected to Persian rule along its northern coastal areas. Thus began the reign of the Al Bu Said, which continues to this day.

Over time, first the British and Dutch and then the French, Germans and Russians became interested in Oman and the Arabian Gulf and, towards the end of the 19th Century CE, in order to protect its trading route to India, Britain signed a series of protectorate treaties with, among others, the Sultan of Muscat and Oman. These treaties remained fully in place until Britain withdrew its presence from the region in the early 1970s.

Until shortly before Britain's departure, Oman had proved to be one of the most isolationist countries in the region. Slavery prevailed and many almost medieval prohibitions remained in force with the then Sultan, Said bin Taimur, refusing to use the country's oil wealth for any purpose other than strengthening his armed forces. However, in 1970, he was deposed in a bloodless coup by his son, Qaboos bin Said, who remains in power today.

In the early years of his reign, HM Sultan Qaboos was faced with guerilla warfare within his country, particularly in the province of Dhofar. Today, all border disputes have been resolved and internal conditions within the country are stable.

Under HM Sultan Qaboos, immense progress has been made in developing the country's social and economic infrastructure, including housing, education, communications and health care, all of which had been officially proscribed in earlier years, but nevertheless Oman continues to spend heavily on defence.

Integral to this progress has been the introduction of what has become known as the Basic Statute of the State, which defines, for the first time, the organs of State. Promulgated in 1996, the Statute provides for a Council of Oman, comprising a Consultative Council and a Council of State – the former being an elected body comprising 82 members, two of whom are women, and the latter an appointed body comprising prominent Omanis in the fields of politics, business and academia. A Defence Council was subsequently established by royal decree, one role of which is to confirm the appointment of a successor as head of state, as predetermined by the present Sultan, in the event that the ruling family proved unable to agree a successor within three days of the throne becoming vacant.

Administratively, the major affairs of the country are in the hands of a number of ministers, with the Sultan at their head as prime minister and, internally, the country is divided into eight governorates, comprising 59 provinces (wilayat), each of which is under the aegis of a provincial governor.

Oman is a member of a number of international bodies including the United Nations, the Arab League and the Cooperation Council of the

Arab States of the Gulf, better known as the Gulf Cooperation Council (GCC), along with Bahrain, Kuwait, Qatar, Saudi Arabia and the United Arab Emirates. However, Oman is not a member of either OPEC or OAPEC, although the country does tend to respect their policies.

1.2

The Economy*

Omani Centre for Investment Promotion and Export Development (OCIPED)

The Sultanate of Oman has made immense strides in the 31 years since HM Sultan Qaboos came to power in late 1970, with the economy having been transformed from being substantially dependent on agriculture and fishing (albeit oil had been found and was a major source of government revenue), to one showing all the signs of modernity and diversity. Clear indications of the achievements of past years are the overall growth in GDP from RO104.7 million (US$272.2 million) in 1970, to a figure, according to initial estimates, of RO7,622.8 million (US$19,819 million) in 2000, and the rise in GDP per capita from RO1,596 (US$4,150) to around RO3,200 (US$8,320) over the same period, and despite substantial population growth in the interim. A further achievement has been diversification of the economic base in the country as the non-oil sector's contribution to GDP rose from 31 per cent in 1970 to some 53.4 per cent in 2000. Important elements of such economic growth and of the diversification programme have been the constantly increasing role of the private sector and the special importance attached to Omanization and to the development and training of Omani nationals.

To ensure focused national development, the Omani government introduced a long-term strategic plan known as 'Economic Vision 2020' within the framework of which a series of Five-Year Development Plans are being implemented. The Fifth Five-Year Plan was the first to be fulfilled under this strategic plan and today the Sixth Plan, covering the period 2001–2005, is in its second year of implementation. According to remarks made by Ahmed bin Abdulnabi Macki, Minister of National Economy and Deputy Chairman of the Financial Affairs and Energy Resources Committee, late in 2001, the goals of the Sixth Plan have been progressing as targeted, with a growth in GDP of 5.9 per cent in the first half of that year, integral to which was growth of 9.9 per cent in the non-oil sectors.

---

*Rate of exchange: RO1 = US$2.6

The minister has also confirmed that the objectives set for 'Economic Vision 2020' had been satisfactorily realized during the Fifth Five-Year Plan, the achievements of which included:

- 6.9 per cent annual average of the actual growth rate of the national economy: well above a targeted average of 4.6 per cent. This was achieved despite the unfavourable conditions which prevailed during 1998–1999 following the steep decline in oil prices and the recession which hit the South-east Asian economies.

- The share of the non-oil sector in GDP rose to 52 per cent, with an actual recorded growth rate of 3.5 per cent. The figures would indicate that the economic diversification programme is being steadily implemented in accordance with the defined, long-term strategy, which has clearly targeted the non-oil sectors for realization of economic diversification.

- A number of strategic projects have been implemented, including the LNG plant in Sur; the expansion of Salalah container terminal; and the development of Sohar port. These are of prime importance to economic diversification and have helped to boost national income and hard-currency earnings.

- Major advances have been secured in the fields of basic, technical and higher education and vocational training. Manpower development is considered a primary element in the country's economic vision, confirmation of which is the recognition of Oman by the World Bank as being one of the major national spenders on education.

- The large expansion in infrastructural and advanced health services, the ultimate benefits of which are best recognized through statistical indicators, which gauge progress in health service provision. The life expectancy rate has risen dramatically to 74 years of age and the incidence of child death rates has dropped to 18 per 1,000 – these figures place Oman on a par with advanced countries in this regard.

- Necessary arrangements for the growth of the private sector and for enhancing its contribution to the national economy were made, including institutional and legal frameworks; improvement of the investment environment; and opening up of the economy to embrace globalization. These moves have resulted in a very tangible contribution to Oman's economic activities by private businesses. Private investment as a percentage of total investment has increased considerably from 28 per cent at the end of the 1980s to more than 40 per cent at the end of the Fifth Five-Year Plan. Projections suggest that private-sector investment will reach 54 per cent of the total investment projected in the Sixth Five-Year Plan, thereby exceeding government investments for the first time.

In 2000, Oman acceded to the World Trade Organization (WTO), a step widely perceived in the Sultanate to be markedly advantageous economically while also creating numerous challenges – not least enhanced competition for national industries. To ensure accession, significant steps were taken by the government to amend the country's legal framework to comply with WTO requirements while continuing to encourage enhanced local and foreign investment; improved productivity and efficiency; reduced costs of production; and increased competitiveness, while observing international standards and specifications.

On a practical level, the government has adopted a number of measures in seeking to diversify sources of national income. These have included the establishment of the Omani Centre for Investment Promotion and Export Development (OCIPED) – see Chapter 5.8; the provision of necessary finance; the granting of priority for lending to export-oriented industries; taking measures to increase productivity in agriculture, fishing and manufacturing industry; and endeavouring to upgrade investment and taxation laws and to streamline government procedures with the aim of attracting additional foreign capital and expertise.

Increased attention is also being given to tourism, in which sector immense potential is foreseen given the country's natural, cultural and heritage resources. Foreign and local private-sector investment is deemed essential to future success in drawing tourists to the Sultanate (see Chapter 1.5).

Integral to the government's economic diversification programme is the privatization policy, which has seen increased Omani and foreign private-sector participation in a number of fields, including electricity generation, water production and port and airport development and management. Further such investment in a number of productive sectors formerly under government control is also predicted (see Chapter 3.3).

In the early years of a new century, Oman finds itself in a very positive economic environment with its basic infrastructure either in place or being developed and a comprehensive, transparent regulatory regime that has inspired confidence in the nation's future among investors worldwide. This is not to suggest that Oman is now resting on its laurels, but instead indicates that the Sultanate is well placed to derive maximum benefit from future economic development in the region.

1.3

Oil, Gas and Petrochemicals

Gregory R Greenwell, Head of Corporate Communications, Petroleum Development Oman[1] (PDO)

Past

The Sultanate of Oman's evolution into a successful oil- and gas-producing nation can be said to have begun in 1937, when Sultan Said bin Taimur granted to the Iraq Petroleum Company (IPC) a 75-year concession covering the entirety of his dominion. The exploration and production operations were to be run on behalf of the IPC by Petroleum Development (Oman and Dhofar) Ltd. The operating company had four shareholders, each with an interest of 23.75 per cent: the Royal Dutch/Shell Group, the Anglo-Persian Company (which would eventually become British Petroleum, or BP), Compagnie Française des Pétroles (CFP, whose convoluted lineage would make it a predecessor of today's TotalFina-Elf) and the Near East Development Company (whose likewise convoluted lineage would make it a subsidiary of today's ExxonMobil). The remaining 5 per cent stake was held by a fifth shareholder, Partex.

With little or no infrastructure to provide water, food, shelter and transport in Oman's hostile desert environment, the early explorers confronted hard times. Problems were compounded by the prevailing belligerency, both domestic (between warring tribes) and international (between the Allied and Axis nations of World War II).

The first well in Oman was finally drilled in early 1956, at Fahud. It was dry. Further wells were drilled, but the only oil discovered – at Marmul – was judged to be too heavy and viscous to be produced

---

[1] The opinions expressed in this article are purely the author's; they do not necessarily reflect those of his employer.

economically. This lack of success, combined with worsening logistical problems and a glut of oil on the world market, led most of the partners to withdraw from the venture in 1960. Only Shell and Partex opted to remain in Oman to continue the search for oil. Their undying optimism, however, was soon to pay off: they struck oil at Yibal in 1962.

When, in 1963, the Natih field was discovered, followed closely by success at Fahud (only a few hundred metres from that dry first well), investment in all the hardware necessary to transport and export Oman's crude could be made. A 276-kilometre pipeline was laid, and an industrial complex at Saih al Maleh (later re-named Mina al Fahal) was built. The first export of Omani oil took place on 27 July 1967.

A month before, CFP rejoined the partnership by taking over two-thirds of Partex's equity share, resulting in the following shareholding in the company that by then had changed its name to Petroleum Development (Oman): Shell 85 per cent, CFP 10 per cent and Partex 5 per cent.

Throughout the 1970s, PD(O) strove to maintain its production and replace its reserves. Some significant discoveries early in the decade contributed to that objective, but it was the oil price hike in 1973 that gave the company a new lease of life because it greatly improved the economics of producing oil in remote locations. Indeed, the Marmul field, rejected originally as uneconomical, was now shown to be commercially viable upon reappraisal.

The first half of the 1970s was also important for a number of other reasons. On 23 July 1970, HM Sultan Qaboos succeeded his father as ruler of the country. On 1 January 1974, the Omani government acquired a 25 per cent shareholding in PD (O); six months later the shareholding was increased to 60 per cent, backdated to the beginning of the year. As a result, the foreign interest in PD(O) comprised Shell (34 per cent), CFP (4 per cent) and Partex (2 per cent). These shareholdings (mutatis mutandis with respect to CFP) have remained unchanged to the present day. However, the company underwent a change on 15 May 1980 when it was registered by royal decree as a limited liability company under the name of Petroleum Development Oman – now without parentheses in its name.

In the early 1980s, production rose to record levels, dispelling doubts about the future of Oman's oil industry. Indeed, the experience it had gained over two decades gave the country enough confidence to venture into the downstream sector of the industry. Beginning in 1982, some of the crude oil reaching Mina al Fahal was diverted to a refinery built at the site. Since that time, the refinery, which is operated by the Oman Refinery Company (ORC), has been meeting most of the domestic demand for petroleum products, including gasoline and jet fuel.

Meanwhile, PDO had also become involved in setting up the Government Gas System. In 1978, the Omani government requested PDO to construct a processing plant and a 345-kilometre, 20-inch pipeline to bring non-associated gas (i.e., gas from gas fields rather than oil fields) from Yibal to Al Ghubra on the coast, where it fuelled a power and desalination plant. On 28 October 1979, HM Sultan Qaboos officially opened the Government Gas Plant at Yibal, ushering in what was to become Oman's important second string in the energy game: its gas industry.

Subsequently, PDO continued to expand the government's gas infrastructure. In 1980, a plant was opened at Yibal to produce the propane and butane that serve as the cooking gas for the country. In 1981, the main gas line was extended via a 230-kilometre, 16-inch pipeline along the Batinah coast to Sohar. At the same time, plants for extraction of liquids from associated gas – a by-product of oil production – were constructed in Yibal, Fahud and Saih Rawl.

In 1984, PDO's involvement in the country's gas industry moved further 'upstream'. An agreement was signed whereby PDO would search specifically for non-associated gas fields on behalf of the government. This gas exploration campaign soon proved highly successful, notching up major discoveries at Saih Nihayda, Saih Rawl and Barik. At the end of 1987, the Sultanate's total non-associated gas reserves stood at 5 trillion cubic feet, and by the end of 1993 they had grown to 18 trillion cubic feet.

When PDO's gas exploration campaign made it clear how bountiful the country's gas fields were, the government decided to establish a completely new industry: the exportation of Liquified Natural Gas (LNG). In 1996, PDO concluded an agreement with the government to develop the central Oman gas fields in order that they might supply gas to an LNG plant in Qalhat, near Sur. The Qalhat plant was to be built and run by a joint-venture company owned mostly by the government but also by several foreign entities, the foremost among them being the Royal Dutch/Shell Group.

To fulfil its part of the agreement, PDO had to drill wells, hook them up to a new gas-processing plant at Saih Rawl, and then transport the processed gas via a 352-kilometre pipeline to Qalhat. For its part, the Oman LNG (OLNG) joint-venture company had to secure long-term purchase commitments from customers and construct the liquefaction plant.

The entire LNG project – including both its upstream and downstream components – cost in excess of US$3 billion, easily earning the title of the single largest industrial project in the Sultanate's history. Moreover, it was executed as planned: the Saih Rawl Central Processing Plant and the gas pipeline to Qalhat were commissioned in November 1999; the first downstream cargo of LNG was shipped to Korea in April 2000; and HM Sultan Qaboos officially opened the LNG plant six months later.

Present

Beginning in the 1980s, a few other exploration and production companies managed to secure licences for the prospecting of land that had been relinquished by PDO since 1937. Some, such as Japex (owned by a Japanese-Indonesian conglomerate) and Occidental of the United States, even scored a few modest successes in finding and developing oil fields. Encouraged by the Omani government, local subsidiaries of the Australia-based Novus Petroleum, the Denmark-based AP Moeller and the US-based Hunt Oil signed more such concession agreements in 2001.

Nevertheless, the upstream part of the oil and gas industry in Oman continues to be dominated by PDO. The company accounts for more than 90 per cent of the Sultanate's 900,000 or so barrels per day of exported crude. (The crude is additionally blended with approximately 70,000 barrels per day of the liquid condensate produced primarily from PDO's central Oman gas fields.) By the end of 2000, its proven oil reserves had reached 5.5 billion barrels.

PDO's achievement has come at the cost of an intense and sustained exploration and field-development effort, particularly during the 1980s and 1990s. During the period 1967–1980, all of PDO's production came from 11 fields; by 1988, 50 fields provided the sum total of PDO's oil output; by 1990 it was 60; and by 1999 it was nearly 100. The achievement has also taxed PDO's technical know-how and innovation.

The ORC refinery has also been hard at work over the years to expand its capacity. It has managed to increase throughput by 70 per cent, from 50,000 barrels per day to 85,000 barrels per day. In 2000, ORC spun off its marketing arm as the Al Maha Petroleum Marketing Company, to compete head-to-head against market stalwarts Shell Oman Marketing and BP Oman.

Still not satisfied with the 21 trillion cubic feet of proven gas reserves that PDO had booked by the end of 2000, the government injected an additional US$10 million spread out over five years into its gas exploration programme. The additional investment has already paid off. Two substantial gas discoveries – at Kauther and Khazzan – were made in 2001. Kauther is credited with 1.25 trillion cubic feet of gas, helping to raise the company's proven gas reserves to 24.5 trillion cubic feet at the start of 2002. Khazzan is still being appraised, but the indications are that it will add even more than Kauther to the nation's gas reserves.

Exports of LNG have been proceeding as planned. They are expected to account for at least 10 per cent of Oman's GDP over the next 25 years.

Future

In spite of its stated vision of producing a million barrels of oil per day, PDO has had to face the fact that for the last three years in a row it has fallen short of its more modest black-oil production targets in the range of 840,000–850,000 barrels per day. It has now come to the realization that its long-standing strategy of developing fields – even if they are small – by drilling wells – even if they are many – has been yielding diminishing returns. PDO has therefore begun directing more attention to optimizing production from existing fields through existing wells. This redirection in strategy extends to the implementation of several enhanced oil-recovery techniques, including steam injection. The focus of the company will thus shift over the next few years from cost cutting to maximizing the recovery of oil.

The Ministry of Oil and Gas also hopes to stimulate the oil and gas industry by attracting more foreign investors to Oman's oil and gas industry. It really is anybody's guess as to what will happen beyond 2012, after the expiry of PDO's concession agreement (which covers an area of nearly 114,000 square kilometres), but if current policy is a guide, then it is likely that the government will favour opening up further opportunities for international oil companies.

Construction of the country's second refinery, at Sohar, is expected to be complete by 2006. It is intended primarily to convert residual products into higher-value products. An associated polypropylene unit is also under consideration.

Without question, however, the country's most ambitious plans revolve around natural gas. For one thing, domestic demand for that fuel is expected to increase as new power plants are constructed to keep up with the growth in demand of electricity. In addition, OLNG is seeking to add a third processing train to its Qalhat plant, thereby increasing the plant's total capacity to almost 10 million tonnes of LNG per year. In any case, a substantial expansion of the country's gas production and distribution infrastructure will be required to bring into reality several envisioned gas-based projects: a fertilizer plant, an aluminium smelter and a methanol plant, to name but a few.

It is in this context that Oman has agreed to participate in the Dolphin gas project, which may one day supply Omani industry with Qatari gas through an Emirati distribution system. Momentum in the project has dissipated somewhat, however, and the recent gas discoveries, in addition to delays in the realization of the Sultanate's gas-fuelled industrial projects, may keep Oman from taking an active part until 2015.

1.4

Commercial Environment: A Market Base on the Indian Ocean Rim

Omani Centre for Investment Promotion and Export Development (OCIPED)

Introduction

One of the most progressive countries in the Middle East, the Sultanate of Oman has worked at creating the right climate for business growth and expansion by developing a free and competitive economy with equal opportunities for all, and by shaping laws that encourage enterprise.

A stable and far-sighted government lies behind all that Oman has to offer. The Omani Rial is pegged to the US dollar and is freely convertible. Liberal investor-friendly policies have been implemented, while procedures for clearances and approval have been simplified. Education and vocational training have been given priority, to ensure that a professionally trained workforce is being developed. The abundant local labour supply can be harnessed and trained to specific requirements. In addition, investors have easy access to a skilled and disciplined external workforce.

Attractive incentives

Investors in Oman enjoy incentives that include:

- up to 100 per cent foreign ownership;
- provision of soft loans with low interest rates and easy payback periods;

- exemption from customs duty on imported plant and equipment;
- relief from customs duty on raw materials for up to 10 years;
- no personal income tax;
- corporate tax holiday of up to 10 years;
- full repatriation of capital, net profit and royalties;
- export credit insurance through the Export Guarantee and Financing Agency.

Opportunities

An abundant supply of energy, relatively low labour costs and inexpensive long-term use of land for industrial purposes are just a few more reasons for wanting to do business in the Oman.

Natural resources offer a variety of industrial possibilities. Oman has large reserves of natural gas that already feed major projects such as Oman LNG (OLNG). This plentiful supply of gas can be made available as a source of energy to various polyolefin and aluminium projects, or as a feedstock to other industries.

At Salalah in the Dhofar region in the south of Oman, an exciting and innovative Free Trade Zone of over 2,400 hectares is planned. To be developed in multiple phases, it will offer a mix of industrial, light manufacturing, logistics and distribution facilities and services, in addition to providing a full package of office, retail, hotel, golf resort and housing amenities.

Phase One of the development will provide customers with over 400,000 square metres of distribution, logistics, freight forwarding and manufacturing facilities.

Salalah's strategic location means that it is ideally positioned for companies wishing to serve both the Gulf and Indian Ocean Rim markets as well as providing fast access to more distant markets such as North America.

Tourism as an industry is gaining ground in the Sultanate. Its unique topography, rich marine life and ancient heritage all offer a fascinating range of activities and sights. Each year Oman attracts increasing numbers of tourists. The government is actively engaged in expanding and developing tourism in the Sultanate, and is seeking private-sector participation in a number of related projects.

Other sectors in which there is perceived to be considerable potential are agriculture, fisheries and interrelated processing industries and mineral extraction and processing.

Substantial areas of Oman are given over to agriculture, particularly along the Batinah coast and in Dhofar in the south – the main crops being dates, bananas and vegetables. Fishing in the rich waters of the Gulf of Oman and the Arabian Sea has been practised for centuries and today has become increasingly important. Integral to pursuit of both activities is a strong desire to develop processing industries in the country.

Oman is widely believed to enjoy substantial mineral wealth, which has been little exploited to date. Thus, the government is seeking to introduce a more liberal and flexible Mining Code than has been in place in the past, which, together with very attractive proposed incentives, is expected to encourage greater local and foreign private-sector investment. Surveys have indicated wide availability of many minerals, both metallic and non-metallic, and the government is seeking not only their exploitation but also the establishment of refining and processing industries and the manufacture of mineral-related products.

1.5

Tourism: Oman – The Essence of Arabia

*Mohsin bin Khamis Al-Balushi,
Under-Secretary of Tourism, Ministry
of Commerce and Industry, Muscat*

Geographically situated at the southern tip of the Arabian Peninsula, the Sultanate of Oman has celebrated a long history and is home to the famous Sinbad legends. Referred to as the 'Essence of Arabia', Oman is a pervading contrast with a fabulous diversity of natural and cultural attributes.

Oman's splendours are not simply restricted to the capital area of Muscat, Muttrah and Ruwi, but also comprise mountain, desert and coast, which combine to create a land of unspoiled beauty where one can take advantage of clean beaches, high mountains and golden desert while following a variety of outdoor pursuits.

Oman's beautiful landscape and natural heritage are evident across the country, be it touching the tip of a rugged mountain or descending into a blue valley; birdwatching on the island of Masirah or catching sight of the egg-laying turtles at Sur; crossing the long carpet of sand at Wahiba; or enjoying the mixture of green and brown colours in the coconut-growing lands of Salalah. All in all, Oman offers a blend of traditional and modern culture and, most of all, a warm and hospitable people.

Oman is a land of hidden but numerous treasures. There is much more for the curious and the adventurous than that which is initially visible. A well-developed infrastructure, a variety of leisure and adventure sports activities and sophisticated hotels, transport and tour facilities all serve to add glamour to the excitement.

Since the inception of Oman's renaissance in 1970, the country's people have sought progress and prosperity as part of a modern Oman. Today, the Sultanate is strongly committed to the principles of positive and constructive international cooperation.

As Oman has developed, so the government has endeavoured to diversify the national economy. Given the undoubted resources and products that Oman has to offer to tourists, the tourism industry has now become a prime element of the economy. A recent study by international experts has confirmed that what Oman has to offer the tourist responds positively to behavioural trends in global tourism.

While the Omani government has been keen to meet the needs of the international tourism market, it has also been anxious to pursue independent policies and relax rigid procedures in order to best serve the interests of incoming visitors. Thus, to enhance the country's attraction for tourists, it has been agreed with the appropriate local authorities to ease entry procedures, thereby easing the path of that upper element of the tourism market which Oman seeks to attract.

The Omani government is also strongly and positively committed to a policy of attracting foreign investment in tourism projects. It is hoped that such investment will help in achieving desired economic diversification, the creation of new job opportunities, the transfer of technology and the development of technical, managerial and marketing skills.

In light of this, special attention is directed to attracting foreign investors' participation in financing such projects as:

Al Sawadi tourism project

The Al Sawadi tourism project is located at Al Sawadi in the province (wilayat) of Baraka, with a total allocated area of approximately 34 square kilometres. The Ministry of Commerce and Industry has supervised the preparation of the feasibility study and the master plan for the project and, early in 2002, was actively promoting the project among specialized international investors.

Daba hotel project

In line with the continuous efforts of the Ministry of Commerce and Industry to establish tourist facilities in various regions of the Sultanate, a four-star hotel project is being planned for Daba province. In conjunction with the Ministry of Housing, Electricity and Water, an area of 50,000 square metres has been allocated to the project, which is being promoted among both local and foreign investors.

Khasab hotel project

In view of the excellent tourist location of Musandam governorate, the Ministry of Commerce and Industry is planning a three-star hotel in Khasab province. The land for the project, an area of 18,887 square metres at Dahar Qainah, is already registered in the name of the Ministry, and the Omani private sector is being encouraged to invest in the project.

In addition, several studies have been and are being conducted in compliance with the government's aim to improve and develop the tourism sector.

The Ministry of Commerce and Industry has commissioned an international consultancy to prepare a master plan, to recommend priorities for developing the tourism sector and to identify five main areas that should be targeted for investment. In February 2002, the study had entered its final phase before completion.

A British company entrusted with preparing a tourism marketing strategy has successfully completed its study and has formulated a well-defined vision for marketing Oman as a tourist destination. The study also determined the role of the private sector in the development of tourism.

Situated in a prime location, Oman is hoping to encourage increasing numbers of tourists to discover and experience a land of nature, hospitality and warmth – the 'Essence of Arabia'.

Part 2

Establishing a Business

Business Structures

Sean Angle and Brian Howard, Trowers &
Hamlins, Muscat

When conducting business in the Sultanate of Oman, several structures can be utilized. Each structure has its relative pros and cons, and considerable thought should be given prior to going ahead and setting up any particular entity.

Commercial agency

The medium of the commercial agent under the Commercial Agencies Law allows a foreign entity to offer its goods for sale in Oman. Use of a commercial agency has the benefit of not having a taxable presence in Oman. However, if the foreign entity exercises too much control of the agent, it is possible that the authorities in Oman will take the view that a point of sale, and therefore a permanent establishment for tax purposes, has been created. Under a commercial agency, the agent will sell on his own account.

Agency contracts should be registered at the Ministry of Commerce and Industry. Difficulties are often encountered when terminating commercial agencies and advice should always be taken on this at the outset of any such arrangement. It is important to note that this cannot be used as a method of obtaining or meeting a foreign entity's requirement of a presence in Oman.

General and limited partnership

Partnerships established under Omani law are separate juristic entities from the parties that form them. A partnership is treated as an incorporated business in the same way as companies are and, consequently, they must be registered. There are two types of partnership: a general partnership and a limited partnership. In a general partnership, the liability of all of the partners is unlimited. In a limited partnership, there can be both general and limited partners. A limited partner's liability is limited to his contribution to the capital of the business.

Joint-stock company

In Oman, there are two types of joint-stock company: the closed joint-stock company (SAOC), and the open or general joint-stock company (SAOG).

The SAOC does not offer its shares to the public, whereas the SAOG must offer a minimum of 40 per cent of its shares to the public unless it has been granted an exemption. This exemption can only be given through a royal decree, because the rule is itself by way of royal decree. SAOCs and SAOGs must be formed by at least three natural or juristic founder members unless formed by the Omani government. In the case of an SAOG, the invitation to the public to subscribe for its shares must be set out in a prospectus which complies with the regulations of the Muscat Securities Market (MSM)/Capital Market Authority (CMA). Subscription must be arranged through at least three banks licensed to operate in the Sultanate.

Shares in a joint-stock company have a nominal value of RO1 (US$2.60) and carry equal rights. However, it is possible to set up different classes of shares within a company whereby certain shares are entitled to enhanced participation in voting and dividends provided that all shares in the same class rank equally.

The management of a joint-stock company is entrusted to a board of directors. An SAOC must have at least three directors and an SAOG five. The maximum number of directors for all joint-stock companies is 12. Directors have maximum terms of office of three years subject to re-election and any person holding 10 per cent of the company's shares has an automatic right to be, or to appoint, a director of that company.

The form and structure of the board of directors and arrangements regarding general meetings of shareholders are subject to detailed regulatory provisions beyond the scope of this chapter, but for which it is important to be prepared when considering the joint-stock company option.

A joint-stock company must file audited accounts with the Ministry of Commerce and Industry and the MSM within three months of the end of the company's financial year. These are open for public inspection and must be approved at the company's AGM.

The minimum levels of share capital for an SAOG and an SAOC are RO2 million and RO500,000, respectively. At least 50 per cent of the issued capital of an SAOC must be paid up on incorporation and the balance must be paid within three years. Any non-cash consideration may be valued by the Ministry of Commerce and Industry and any shortfall will have to be made up. In addition, joint-stock companies are required to establish a 'legal reserve' using 10 per cent of the company's annual net profit. However, once this legal reserve amounts to one-third of the company's capital, the requirement to set aside profits expires. The legal reserve cannot be distributed as dividend.

The CMA has introduced new disclosure norms for SAOGs in order to bring regulation in line with accepted international best practices. The CMA's primary concern is that companies taking advantage of public investment are fully accountable for that.

Shareholders' agreements are not uncommon between members of an SAOC. These often detail attendance requirements, percentages of votes and minority shareholders' rights.

Limited liability company (LLC)

The establishment of a limited liability company (LLC) is relatively easy and quick. It is cheaper than establishing an SAOG/SAOC. An LLC is also entitled to conduct full commercial operations in Oman, but it should be noted that the objects of an LLC must be limited to a specific area of business or trade, unlike an SAOC which can have 'general' business or trade as its object.

An LLC is less regulated than an SAOG/SAOC. There are fewer reporting requirements and in certain cases an LLC need not appoint an auditor. It is easier also to operate on a daily basis – for example, an LLC can pass members' resolutions in writing without holding a meeting, whereas this is not possible for an SAOG/SAOC.

An LLC must have a minimum of two and a maximum of 40 participants. All shares in an LLC must be fully paid up and of the same nominal value. The management of an LLC is through a manager or managers rather than through a board of directors. Under the terms of the company's constitutive contract (akin to articles of association), the day-to-day running of the company and many of the decisions taken in the ordinary course of business can be delegated to the manager(s).

A manager can be removed by a decision at a shareholders' meeting. The company will be bound by all acts performed by its managers acting in its name and within the scope of their authority.

In contrast to joint-stock companies' and shareholders' rights to appoint directors, a member of an LLC has no right to be, or to appoint, a manager. The LLC structure suits a small operation with a limited number of promoters and is more akin to a partnership. However, the nature of an LLC can be brought closer to that of a joint-stock company by way of a members' agreement between the LLC and its members. Such agreements are often used to implement a control structure similar to an SAOC's board of directors.

The minimum share capital for an LLC in Oman is RO20,000. However, under the Foreign Capital Investment Law (FCIL), a foreign company will not be able to obtain an interest in an Omani company unless its share capital amounts to at least RO150,000. There are additional specific requirements and limitations in respect of the percentage of shares that a foreign owner may hold in an Omani company. These are beyond the scope of this chapter, but are detailed in Chapter 2.2.

The contribution to capital can be in cash or kind, but cannot include the services or labour of any person. The capital must be paid into a special account in the LLC's name at an Omani-licensed bank. The capital of an LLC can be increased or reduced by unanimous resolution of the shareholders, but the capital may not be reduced below RO150,000. LLCs cannot resort to direct or indirect public subscription in raising/increasing capital or funds. A company's capital must be contributed in full before it is established.

If a company's capital exceeds RO50,000 it must have at least one independent auditor. However, in practice a company will require this for tax returns in any event. Within four months following the end of the financial year, the company must prepare accounts and auditors' reports (where relevant). Shareholders may act through resolutions adopted at meetings. In general, resolutions are carried by simple majority with a few exceptions (e.g., altering a company's constitution or share capital).

The words 'with limited liability' or 'LLC' must follow the name of the company. Shares are not divisible but can be jointly owned. The company must maintain a Shareholder Register detailing names, addresses, nationalities and number of shares owned by each member. No person will be considered as owner of the shares until his name has been entered into the Shareholder Register. Pre-emption rights exist in favour of existing shareholders of an LLC should a shareholder wish to assign his shares to a third party. Shares attract one vote each. A quorum is constituted if half of the company's shareholders are in attendance at a general meeting, although this can be altered through the company's constitutive contract.

Branch office

A foreign (i.e., non-Omani) company which has entered into a contract with a government entity or quasi-government entity (such as Petroleum Development Oman (PDO), or Oman LNG (OLNG)) is entitled to register and operate in Oman on a branch office basis. The branch registration is dependent on the term of the government contract, which must also be registered, and its purpose is to carry out the contract.

The branch office is not entitled to seek and carry out business with the private sector. It should be noted that foreign branches are treated for tax purposes as 100 per cent foreign owned.

Commercial representative office (CRO)

Commercial representative offices (CROs) are relatively new to Oman, having been permissible only since 2000. The function of a representative office is primarily to liaise with and form new contacts with clients in both the public and private sectors, with the aim of introducing a company's products and expanding the market for such products. CROs may not import goods (except samples for marketing), sell products in Oman or promote products or services other than those originating from the representative company. The CRO's tasks are to liaise, market and monitor, but not to trade.

Registration is required with the Commercial Register at the Ministry of Commerce and Industry. Due to its novelty, the structure of a CRO is quite cumbersome. The company being represented must have been registered for a continuous period of 10 years with at least three foreign branch offices registered in different jurisdictions. Registration of a CRO is valid for a period of five years on payment of certain fees.

Contractual joint venture

A contractual joint venture is mandated for in the Commercial Companies Law (CCL) but does not give rise to a corporation. Instead, it is considered as a separate taxable entity for the purposes of the Tax Law.

The future

Oman is very much in a 'watch this space' phase at present, as the authors of this chapter have it on very good authority that the CCL is currently being redrafted. The object of the redraft is to create corporate entities which will be more familiar and therefore more acceptable to international investors.

2.2

Legalities, Policies and Procedures

*Sean Angle and Nicholas Green, Trowers &
Hamlins, Muscat*

Introduction

Non-Omanis wishing to do business in Oman should be aware of the
sources of law governing the regulation of their business. The Commercial Companies Law (CCL), Royal Decree 4/1974, as amended, and the
Commercial Register Law, Royal Decree 3/1974, govern business entities
in Oman. Recent amendments to the CCL provide for more sophisticated
and efficient corporate structures and encourage wider share ownership
and public participation in joint-stock companies.

The Foreign Capital Investment Law (FCIL), Royal Decree 102/1994,
governs the participation of non-Omani nationals in a trade or business
in Oman. The law specifies capital requirements and levels of Omani
participation in capital and profits.

Types of business structure

Although this issue is specifically addressed in Chapter 2.1, there follows
a brief reminder of the types of business structure available to the
foreign investor.

Commercial agency

A foreign entity may offer its goods for sale in Oman without having a
taxable presence in the country, by use of the medium of a commercial
agent. The agent must operate independently of the foreign principal.
If the foreign entity exercises too much control over the agent, it is
possible that the authorities will take the view that a point of sale, and
therefore a permanent establishment for tax purposes, has been created.
The agency contract should be registered at the Ministry of Commerce

and Industry. The commercial agency structure is discussed in more detail in Chapter 6.2.

General and limited partnership

Partnerships established under Omani law are separate legal entities from the partners that form them. They are treated as incorporated businesses in the same way as companies and as such need to be registered. In a general partnership, the liability of all partners is unlimited. The limited partnership distinguishes between general and limited partners, with the latter partners' liability being limited to their contribution to the capital.

Joint-stock company

A joint-stock company must be formed by at least three founder members (natural or juristic persons), whose liability is limited to the nominal value of their shares in the company's capital. Companies formed by the government solely or jointly with others are exempt from this requirement. If at least 40 per cent of a company's shares are issued for public subscription, it is considered a general joint-stock company (SAOG); if a company's shares are not issued for public subscription, it is considered a closed joint-stock company (SAOC). Shares have a nominal value of RO1 and carry equal rights. It is possible to have different classes of shares, providing for enhanced voting rights or profits, provided that all shares of a similar nature have equal rights. Companies seeking to conduct insurance, banking or commercial air transportation businesses must be organized in the form of joint-stock companies.

Limited liability company (LLC)

An LLC must have a minimum of two and a maximum of 40 participants. All shares must be fully paid up and of the same nominal value (RO1). An LLC is less regulated than an SAOG/SAOC. The reporting requirements are also less onerous than for an SAOG/SAOC and in certain cases an auditor need not be appointed.

An LLC is generally easier to operate on a daily basis. For example, management of an LLC is through a manager or managers rather than through a board of directors. Under the terms of the company's constitutive contract, the day-to-day running of the company and many of the decisions taken in the ordinary course of business can be delegated to the manager(s). Such a structure suits a small operation with a limited number of promoters more akin to a partnership. A control structure, similar to the board of directors of an SAOC/SAOG, can be introduced by way of an agreement between the members of an LLC. Establishment of an LLC is also an easier and quicker process, and therefore cheaper, than the establishment of an SAOG/SAOC.

Branch office

A foreign company which has entered into a contract with a government entity or quasi-government entity is entitled to register and operate in Oman as a foreign branch.

Foreign commercial representative office

Under Ministerial Decision 22/2000, foreign companies and establishments engaged in the trade, industry and service sectors may open commercial representative offices in Oman

Foreign Capital and Investment Law (FCIL)

Whether a foreign company intends to trade or invest on its own account or as a partner with an Omani company, the effect of the Commercial Code and the FCIL is that the activity of the foreign company is unlawful unless the appropriate authorizations have been issued by the Ministry of Commerce and Industry. All companies with foreign participation must also obtain licences from the Committee for the Investment of Foreign Capital ('the Committee').

There is no such thing as an 'off the shelf' company in Oman. Every company must be specifically incorporated and is subject to express authorization in respect of any foreign investor. This is neither a simple nor speedy process and requires the preparation of a significant amount of documentation on the part of the foreign shareholder.

Oman's restrictions on foreign ownership do not apply in the same way to Gulf Cooperation Council (GCC) nationals investing in or pursuing activities in certain areas, including industry, agriculture, construction, the retail and wholesale trade, the hotel and restaurant business (Ministerial Decision 25/1984), among others. This is pursuant to its GCC treaty obligations, although the Sultanate reserves specified conditions that must be met for GCC nationals to invest in and pursue activities in these areas.

FCIL licence

Article 1 of the FCIL provides that non-Omanis may not acquire an interest in the capital of an Omani company without a licence to do so obtained from the Ministry of Commerce and Industry. Article 2 of the FCIL sets out the conditions to be met for obtaining such a licence. The first of these is that the company should have a minimum share capital of not less than RO150,000. Higher capital requirements can apply depending on the type of company. Following Royal Decree 39/1998 amending CCL 4/1974, the minima for an SAOC and SAOG respectively are RO500,000 (US\$1.3 million) and RO2 million (US\$5.2 million).

Under Article 2 of the FCIL, the foreign shareholding should not exceed 49 per cent, although it may be increased to 65 per cent if the minister agrees following a recommendation of the Committee. Article 2 also states that it is possible to increase this percentage to 100 for projects which contribute to the development of the national economy, which have a minimum project capital of RO500,000, and which are approved by the Committee following a recommendation by the minister.

Article 5 of the FCIL indicates that the Committee when assessing applications for foreign ownership in excess of 49 per cent should submit its recommendations having regard to a) the type of investment, b) the extent to which the project may be considered 'an economic development project', and c) the priority to be offered to the project. Priority will be given to projects using local products and/or raw materials; projects that assist export, introduce new technology or produce to the country; projects that attempt to attract or relocate industries with international repute; or tourist projects establishing integrated villages and tourist areas. Under a recent Ministerial Decision, priority will now be given to those foreign companies that actively promote 'Omanization' of the workforce.

Approval for a foreign shareholding in excess of 49 per cent remains discretionary. As part of Oman's commitments in joining the World Trade Organization (WTO) in October 2000, the government agreed to raise the ceiling on foreign participation of business entities (with a few minor exceptions) to 70 per cent, effective from 1 January 2001. While amendments have been made to the tax laws in respect of this commitment, no amendments have yet been made to the FCIL although the Ministry of Commerce and Industry has routinely permitted the registration of companies with 70 per cent foreign participation. It is expected that the change will involve receiving approval through a more simplified process than the Committee referred to above.

Registration formalities

In addition to obtaining the FCIL licence, it is necessary to complete registration formalities for the corporate entity at the following governmental departments:

- Company Affairs Department at the Ministry of Commerce and Industry;

- Commercial Registration Department at the Ministry of Commerce and Industry;
- Oman Chamber of Commerce and Industry (OCCI).

Land ownership

Under the Land Law, Royal Decree 5/1980, all land belongs to the State. The Ministry of Housing, Electricity and Water is charged with the responsibility and authority to allocate land and register security over that land. Further pursuant to the Land Law, companies and foreign nationals may not own land except in certain exceptional circumstances. GCC nationals, companies wholly owned by Omanis, and general joint-stock companies with at least 51 per cent Omani shareholding may own land in certain circumstances.

Royal Decree 5/1981 regulates the exploitation of land in Oman by foreigners and companies. Article 1 now provides that the Ministry of Housing, Electricity and Water may grant to a company or a foreign national the right to use a certain property for operations that promote the economic development of Oman. For example, a lease and a right to benefit may be assigned or mortgaged (Article 2). However, unlike a lease, a right to benefit expires on the death of the beneficiary. If the right to benefit is given to a company, it expires on its termination date, which is fixed when the right is first conferred. On expiration of a right to benefit, the beneficiary must be compensated for the value of any improvements constructed during the terms of the right.

The decision by the minister to grant non-Omani or companies where Omani shareholding is less than 51 per cent, the right to benefit from State lands shall be final only after approval by the Council of Ministers.

Royal Decree 5/1981 is amended by Royal Decree 24/1995, Article 4 of which states that the term of the right to benefit should be within the requirements of the project but for not more than 50 years, renewable at the request of the proprietor. This is not outright ownership.

Omanization

The aim of Omanization is to limit the Sultanate's dependence on expatriate staff. Non-Omanis are not permitted to work in Oman unless clearance has been obtained from the Ministry of Manpower. Royal Decree 11/1999 states that employers must employ Omanis wherever possible, and different sectors of industry are given different Omanization percentages which must be met. These range from 15 per cent (contracting) to 60 per cent (transport, storage and communications). Additional Omanization targets are also set by various other government departments – for example, in 2000 the Central Bank of Oman set a 90 per cent Omanization target by the end of the year for banks. Failure to reach industry targets is punishable by a cash fine worked out on the following basis: the fine is equal to 50 per cent of the average total pay of non-Omani workers, which represents the difference between the Omanization percentage which should have been achieved and the percentage actually achieved. Omani labour law is reviewed in more depth elsewhere.

It is important to note that some areas of the economy are, in Oman as elsewhere in the world, more heavily regulated. Particular reference is made here to the banking, insurance and investment sectors, which have additional regulations imposed by the Central Bank of Oman as well as specific Omani legislation. The aim of this chapter is to give a brief overview of the legalities facing all commercial enterprises considering doing business in Oman. More detailed information on setting up in the three above-mentioned sectors appears in Chapter 5.3.

2.3

Industrialization

Dr Hamed H Al Dhahab, Director-General of Industry, Ministry of Commerce and Industry, Ruwi

The social and economic advancement of the Sultanate of Oman over the past two to three decades has been rapid and dramatic. With the advent of oil revenues in the early 1970s, Oman was able to establish a world-class basic infrastructure such as roads, ports, communications and health care facilities, all in a remarkably short period of time. While oil wealth continues to play a significant role in the national economy, the country has also realized the importance of shifting itself away from an economy based solely on oil production to one with diverse income sources.

The issuance of the Royal Decree 1/1979 on Organization and Encouragement of Industry, promulgated in 1979, was the beginning of the process of industrialization in Oman. Then came Royal Decree 40/1987 offering financial support to the private sector in the fields of industry, tourism, health, education, heritage and agriculture. This represented a major step in providing impetus to economic activity in the country and was followed by several progressive policy initiatives aimed at nurturing the industrial sector. Thus, starting with some 10 registered factories in 1975, Oman now has nearly 900 working industrial units.

The country is now preparing itself to meet the challenges in the new millennium through a planned structural transformation in the economy. It is expected that, by 2020, the contribution to GDP by production and services other than oil and gas will rise to 81 per cent.

Early development process

Apart from the policy initiatives aimed at promoting industrialization, a major step that gave impetus to industrial development in Oman was the setting up of the first industrial estate at Rusayl in 1985. The private sector, which by and large represented the trading sector, more or less grasped the opportunity to venture into manufacturing, availing of top-class infrastructure facilities provided by the government at highly concessional rates. Learning from the experience of the Rusayl Industrial Estate, five other industrial estates were subsequently set up in different regions of the country. These estates now accommodate nearly 200 industrial units of varying activities and investment levels (Table 2.3.1). Much later, in 1993, the Public Establishment for Industrial Estates (PEIE) was formed as the apex administrative body for all the industrial estates. This was more or less a consolidation of successful government intervention in providing infrastructure for industrial development.

Industrial estates

The setting-up of industrial estates not only provided direction to potential entrepreneurs but also created ample role models in society, which has had a multiplier effect in industrializing Oman. The subsequent efforts of the government were through fiscal and financial incentives to attract industrial investments. Several policy initiatives, including those facilitating foreign investment, were taken to support the industrial sector and also to make Omani industry competitive. Many industries have thus come into existence even outside the industrial estates. The government's soft loans, duty exemption on the import of raw materials and equipment, and tax holidays were some of the incentives that played a catalytic role in the process of industrialization.

At the same time, efforts were taken to create appropriate value systems in society to support the process of industrialization. The institution of His Majesty's Cup for the Best Industry, starting from 1991, was a significant message to society in terms of the government's priority towards industrialization.

With the naming of 1998 as the Year of the Private Sector, the government expressed its commitment to pursue policies that integrated private industries and businesses with national goals. Accordingly, the government adopted a number of policies and procedures to encourage the private sector, including the privatization of several public projects such as the National Insurance Company, the Oman Hotels Company and the National Bank of Oman and, in January 2002, Seeb International Airport, which is the only international airport in the Sultanate.

Some tangible achievements

Under the long-term development strategy, the efforts of the government have been to intensify the development of the non-oil sectors, thereby

Table 2.3.1 Industrial estates

Name	Date of establishment	Number of units in production	Location	Additional services offered
Rusayl	1985	125	10 kilometres from Seeb International Airport. 45 kilometres from Sultan Qaboos port.	Government office. Medical services. Residential area for staff. Commercial services (cargo office, stationery shop, supermarket and restaurant).
Raysut	1992	13	4 kilometres from Salalah port.	Central laboratory for specification and measurement. Training institute. Gas supply in progress. Free Trade Zone to be established.
Sohar	1992	37	220 kilometres from Dubai, UAE.	Industrial port under construction. Medical centre, residential complex and government office units under construction.
Nizwa	1994	5	Al-Dakhliya region	Plans to build up medical centre, post office and residential area for staff.
Buraimi	1998	13 (12 are under construction)	120 kilometres from Dubai, UAE. 120 kilometres from Sohar. 375 kilometres from Muscat.	Nil.
Qalhat	1999	LNG plant	Sur province (wilayat)	Land area earmarked for recreation, health and housing.

achieving a diversification of the economic base of the country. Due to these efforts, the Sultanate was able to achieve positive developments in the structure of the national economy as the contribution of manufacturing to GDP increased from 0.5 per cent in 1976 to 2.9 per cent in 1990 and then to 5.4 per cent in 2000 (at current prices).

The industrial base of Oman (as of 2000), in terms of the activities under ISIC classification, is shown in Table 2.3.2. Excluding refined petro-products and LNG, the predominant sectors of industrial activity in Oman are non-metallic minerals, food and beverages, garments and fabricated metal products.

Table 2.3.2 Industrial base, 2000

ISIC	Activity	No. of establish-ments	Investment (RO'000)	Number of employees	Production (RO'000)
15	Food and beverages	167	109,530	6420	164,547
18	Readymade garments	22	3,620	6357	39,501
20	Wood products, except furniture	65	1,736	829	6,558
21	Paper products	8	4,171	520	9,801
22	Printed material	36	16,776	1,452	14,985
23	Refined petro-products	10	635,508	987	557,127
24	Chemicals/chemical products	35	31,008	1382	53,748
25	Rubber and plastic products	29	19,882	1270	22,871
26	Other non-metallic products	257	169,128	6286	93,650
27	Basic metals	7	58,329	1023	36,911
28	Fabricated metal products	139	19,586	3910	33,595
29	Machinery and equipment (nec)	18	5,160	573	10,800
30	Office, accounting/computer machinery	2	110	49	623
31	Electrical machinery/apparatus	13	11,806	780	26,510
33	Medical, precision and optical equipment	2	8,971	55	2,524
34	Motor vehicle parts	5	929	81	346
35	Other transport equipment	9	125	41	427
36	Furniture manufacturing	40	7,613	2655	32,446
90	Other manufacturing	12	12,585	644	8,912
	Total	876	1,116,573	35,314	1,115,882

Source: Annual Census Survey, Ministry of Commerce and Industry.

The total number of establishments (having a capital investment of RO5,000 and above) reached a figure of 876 in 2000, compared to 812 in 1997. The corresponding gross value added in the manufacturing sector was RO402 million (US$1,037 million) in 2000 as compared to RO232 million (US$598.6 million) in 1997. These figures indicate a compounded annual growth rate of 2.6 per cent in number of establishments and 20.1 per cent in terms of gross value added. If the contribution from the refined petroleum products and LNG is excluded, the growth rate in value addition would be 5.5 per cent.

Out of the 876 establishments, 411 are small-scale (manpower not exceeding nine), 377 are medium-scale (manpower of 10–99) and 88 are large-scale units (manpower of 100 and above). Figures of the past few years indicate that there has been a decline in the number of small-scale establishments in operation, while the medium and large sectors had more or less the same growth rates. However, of late, the Sultanate has realized the importance of nurturing the small-scale industrial sector, particularly from the point of view of generating employment opportunities. The efforts in this direction would also aim at developing entrepreneurship and self-employment through a programme entitled 'Sanad' (Support).

One of the major achievements of the manufacturing sector has been that it has provided jobs to 11,362 Omanis, representing 32 per cent of the total workforce in the manufacturing sector. About a decade ago, the percentage of Omanis in the industrial sector was less than 15 per cent. The current regulations do stipulate a minimum of 35 per cent Omanization of the workforce in each industrial establishment. The labour productivity in the industrial sector in Oman has always shown an upward trend.

The regional distribution of the units is indicated in Table 2.3.3. The Muscat governorate tops the list, with about 47 per cent of the total number of establishments, 74 per cent of the total employment and 85 per cent of the gross sales.

With regard to the infrastructure build-up relevant to industrial development, Oman now has 8,477 kilometres of paved roads and 25,370

Table 2.3.3 Distribution of industrial activity by region, 2000

Region	Number of establishments	Number of employees	Value added (RO'000)	Finished goods (RO'000)
Muscat governorate	336	24,141	201,437	766,453
Batinah	107	4,754	32,272	81,757
Dhahira	66	2,006	12,204	24,153
Dakhliya	156	1,343	8,277	15,127
Sharkhia	134	1,199	134,138	187,784
Dhofar governorate	77	1,871	13,170	40,548
Total	876	35,314	401,498	1,115,822

Source: Annual Census Survey, Ministry of Commerce and Industry.

kilometres of graded roads. There is a modern international airport, which handles around 38,000 inbound and outbound flights and around 2.7 million passengers per year. Oman's modern seaports and other utilities complement the industrial sector as they act as the export points for national products. The Sultan Qaboos port in Muscat has already been modernized, Salalah container port has been commissioned and Sohar port is under development. Salalah port is also being developed as a Free Trade Zone. This port, which is close to major international container traffic routes between Europe and the Far East, is aimed at making Oman an international re-export centre. Oman is linked by a large and very advanced communications network.

Institutional support

The Ministry of Commerce and Industry, PEIE, Omani Centre for Investment Promotion and Export Development (OCIPED), Oman Development Bank (ODB), Oman Chamber of Commerce and Industry (OCCI) and Muscat Securities Market (MSM) all provide assistance and support to investors in Oman.

OCIPED was established by royal decree in 1996, as an autonomous government organization with the following objectives:

- To act as a facilitator for foreign investors.

- To encourage private-sector investment in the Sultanate.

- To encourage investment in export-oriented manufacturing industry.

- To promote the export of Omani products.

OCCI was established in 1973 in order to promote and protect the economic interests of the country. It has a membership of some 84,000 business establishments. Membership subscriptions and revenues from the services offered to the public form the main sources of financing for this institution.

ODB was established through royal decree in 1997 with the objective of advancing finance to small and medium-sized projects. Furthermore, the Export Credit Guarantee Agency (ECGA) operates under the umbrella of ODB.

MSM, which was set up in 1989, is an important tool and source for financing several industrial and service projects in the country. Total number of public listed companies in the MSM at the end of 2001 was 139, with a market capitalization of RO1,106.7 million.

There have also been significant private initiatives trying to provide all-under-one-one-roof support to budding SME entrepreneurs. The Fund for Development of Youth Projects and the Intilaaqah are the two major initiatives.

The Youth Fund encourages Omani youth to establish SMEs, wherein the fund authorities will assist the entrepreneur from concept to commissioning and also provide managerial guidance, without directly participating in financing the equity of project.

Intilaaqah, on the other hand, works with the objective of stimulating and encouraging young Omanis to consider the option of starting their own businesses and to provide assistance to those who wish to take up that option. Since its inception in 1995, Intilaaqah has trained 319 aspirants, out of whom 71 have started their own businesses.

Investment incentives

Oman has both political and macroeconomic stability. It has a liberal economy based on the principles of an open and free market which is driven by the private sector. The market economy remains the main focus of Oman's strategy since its renaissance. The country is also strategically located on the Indian Ocean.

As part of its efforts to nurture industrial activities and also to attract foreign investments, Oman offers such financial incentives and support as:

- Government soft loans with an interest rate of 3 per cent for investment projects.

- A strong and stable local currency, the Omani Rial (RO1 = US\$2.58), which is fully convertible. Oman's laws allow free transfer of capital funds, profits, and remittances from foreign workers.

- Plant, machinery and spare parts imported for industrial investment are exempted from customs duties. Raw and semi-processed materials imported for manufacturing and which are not available locally are also exempted from paying customs duties.

- Oman's investment laws guarantee exemption from income tax for a five-year period, which may be renewed for another period of five years. Oman does not levy any personal income tax.

- Oman has a liberal Foreign Capital Investment Law (FCIL). This law was further liberalized when the government decided to permit foreign equity up to 70 per cent. Appropriate legislative amendment is being made. Even 100 per cent foreign equity could be permitted by the government in the case of a project being considered vital for development of the national economy.

- In order to promote exports, the Export Guarantee Agency was set up by a decision of the Development Council in 1989 and started functioning in 1991.

- Planned and serviced plots are provided by the government, to set up industrial units. Ready-built factories of various sizes, which can be leased for a period of 25 years (renewable), are also available. Services provided at the industrial estates include roads, water, gas, communication means, liquid waste processing, solid waste collection and disposal etc. The government levies only a nominal rent on the premises at the industrial estates as shown below:

  - Annual rent for land plots = 250 baisas per square metre for the first five years and 500 baisas per square metre after five years;

  - Annual rent for building = OR2.4 per square metre.

- Competitive electricity, water and fuel tariffs for manufacturing, as given below:

  - Electricity = 24 baisas per Kw/h during summer months and 12 baisas per Kw/h during winter months;

  - Water = 3 baisas per gallon;

  - Natural gas = 20.4 baisas per cubic metre.

Foreign investment: a closer look

The Omani government is committed to the policy of attracting foreign investment. It is hoped that this will help achieve economic diversification, transfer of technology, employment generation and the development of technical and managerial capabilities. Special attention is directed to attracting foreign investors participating in megaprojects.

In addition to the favourable laws and regulations on foreign capital investment, the investor also seeks a friendly, supportive and hassle-free environment in which to carry on his business activities. The procedures and processes to be followed before, during and after the implementation of a project are also important factors influencing the judgement and preferences of investors. Keeping this objective in mind, the government established OCIPED to act as a friend, guide and facilitator for investors. Gradually, OCIPED has intensified the pace and depth of investment promotion in Oman by identifying viable opportunities and bringing these to the notice of local and foreign investors in coordination with the government and private organizations. OCIPED has provided facilitation and matchmaking services to many projects in the manufacturing, tourism, fisheries, telecommunications and infrastructure, and IT sectors.

The government has recently adopted the policy of establishing Free Trade Zones in a number of locations in Oman, primarily to exploit the country's strategic location to attract foreign investment. The Free Zones presently being considered are:

- Salalah Port Free Zone.

- Al Mazyouna Free Zone.

While Salalah port has been developed as one of the leading container ports on the Indian Ocean, the Free Trade Zone is aimed at developing Salalah region and turning it into a prosperous regional distribution centre.

After the successful demarcation of the borders between the Sultanate of Oman and Republic of Yemen, trade in the Al Mazyouna region has witnessed consistent growth. It is expected that the establishment of a Free Trade Zone could assist in transforming Al Mazyouna into an active trading location. The first phase of this project will focus on establishing warehouses and branches of both Omani and Yemeni companies. This will be followed by the opening of liaison offices and commercial centres and finally the target will be to attract a number of export-oriented industries into the Zone.

Reasons to invest

Over the next 20 years, the country is looking to attract RO4.5 billion (US$11.6 billion) of investment in industry. Oman is an industrial destination that provides many advantages, including:

- Political stability.

- A law that allows up to 100 per cent foreign capital.

- Freedom to repatriate capital and profits.

- Stable currency with full convertibility.

- Tax holidays up to a maximum of 10 years.

- No personal income tax.

- Free trade and open market policy.

- Strategic location.

- Modern infrastructure.

- Exemption of customs duties on import of plant and machinery and raw materials.

- Determined policy of privatization.

Tax benefits

Foreign investment projects are exempt from tax on profits for a period of five years, renewable for a further five years.

Eligibility for government soft loan

If no more than 49 per cent of the foreign equity is owned by the foreign investor, the project will be eligible for a government soft loan.

Current strategy

Oman's industrial strategy up to 2020 envisages that within a stable macroeconomic framework provided by the government, sustainable development will be attained by using the private sector as the primary engine of growth. A diversified, dynamic and globalized economy is to be established through a strong, efficient and competitive private sector. It is expected that by 2020 the manufacturing sector should be able to contribute 15 per cent of Oman's GDP.

With a relatively small local market, Oman's strategy to achieve the above goals focuses on nurturing export-oriented internationally competitive industries, which are capital-, technology- and knowledge-intensive. Competitiveness is further enhanced by the use of certain locally available raw materials, particularly minerals and the resources of the sea. The country's abundant natural gas will serve as a source of energy and feedstock for many a highly value-added and export-oriented project.

In general, the following types of industry will be encouraged:

- industries utilizing local raw materials;
- export-oriented industries;
- industries using gas as the main source of energy or feedstock;
- capital-, knowledge- and technology-intensive projects;
- projects that employ a large number of Omanis;
- downstream petrochemicals;
- industries that can serve as production centres for multinationals for international marketing of products.

The commissioning of Oman LNG (OLNG) in 1999 represented a major step in the above direction, which would provide impetus to many a gas-based project. The Indo-Oman fertilizer project, another private-sector fertilizer project, a petro-refinery, a methanol plant and an aluminium smelter are some of the major projects that are on the anvil.

The foregoing in no way indicates any constraint on the type of industrial activities in Oman, other than restrictions based on environmental reasons or on account of specific regulations in any particular sector. Industrial licences are therefore provided without any regimentation.

However, manufacturing units have to strictly abide by the regulations on environment, product quality, safety regulations, commercial regulations and labour laws.

New generation strategies

Small business development

Approximately 45 per cent of Oman's population is under 15 years of age, a vast majority of them undergoing some kind of formal education. Therefore, in the years to come, a large number of educated Omanis will become active job-seekers. This prompts the government to take active steps to nurture small enterprises and self-employment ventures. Steps in this direction will also embrace entrepreneurial training. The aforementioned 'Sanad' programme is a deliberate effort in this direction.

IT park

Oman has realized the potential of information and communications technology (ICT) in economic development. In the years to come, substantial steps will be taken to nurture a knowledge-based economy. The first step already initiated in this direction is the IT park, which is being implemented in Rusayl. This park, apart from having ready-to-occupy built-up space available on lease to IT companies, will also have an IT college as a private venture. A business incubator is also being planned to support IT start-ups.

Oman Society for Petroleum Services (OPAL)

Philip Dew, Philip Dew Consultancy Limited, Bahrain

The Oman Society for Petroleum Services (OPAL) was registered early in 2002 following receipt of formal approval from the Council of Ministers. It warrants inclusion here on the basis that it is a unique organization within the Gulf States and wider Arab world. In short, OPAL has been formed to enhance professionalism in Oman at a time when the Sultanate has acceded to the World Trade Organization (WTO) and therefore recognizes the need to fully prepare local businesses for the many challenges that are likely to lie ahead.

OPAL is an industry-wide alliance of oil and gas companies, including oil and gas producers, refiners, marketing companies, contractors and suppliers, be they large or small. The leaders of businesses in these sectors meet monthly at the Oman Chamber of Commerce and Industry (OCCI) to discuss areas of mutual benefit and consensus.

OPAL aims to provide a single umbrella body to agree and promote standards of work competence and professionalism with a view to Oman's oil and gas industry being recognized as world-class. It seeks to embrace and address specific local challenges positively and to seek out innovative and cost-effective solutions that may be welcomed and applied throughout the industry. OPAL has expressed confidence that it can significantly improve communication of best practice, ideas and lessons throughout the industry. In this regard it has focused particularly on Omanization, employment practices, training and development, quality, health, safety and environment, local community relationships and best practices.

With Omanization very much in mind, one of OPAL's first actions has been to enter into a Memorandum of Understanding with the

Ministry of Manpower, under which members of OPAL will recruit, train and employ 1,000 new Omanis in the industry during 2002. This partnership with government is widely and rightly perceived as a programme of national importance.

During January 2002, a formal Code of Practice for OPAL was in the process of finalization.

Part 3

Company Operational Issues

3.1

Legal Aspects of Intellectual Property

Andrew Rae and Brian Howard, Trowers &
Hamlins, Muscat

Oman has been keen to develop this area of law due to the Sultanate's recent entry into the World Trade Organization (WTO) and its membership of the World Intellectual Property Organization (WIPO). Oman is a subscriber to the Paris Convention for the Protection of Industrial Property Rights and the Berne Convention for the Protection of Literary and Artistic Works. Within the past two years there has been a spate of new legislation dealing with the protection of intellectual property. It is notable that the protection of intellectual property rights is carried out through mechanisms very similar to those used in Western jurisdictions and which will be familiar to many business managers.

Trademarks

The Law of Trademarks was updated by Royal Decree 38/2000. This lists in some detail those trademarks that may or may not be registered. Marks cannot be registered if they do not conform with Oman's high standards of decency, are of a purely religious nature, incorporate false information or bear a resemblance to an already established mark or trade name.

In Oman, there is a Register of Trademarks and Trade Names at the Ministry of Commerce and Industry. The procedure for trademark registration involves an initial search of the Register and confirmation of the relevant classes. A sample of the trademark and all relevant information and documentation relating to it will need to be supplied. Once the application is lodged and approved, it is advertised in the *Official Gazette* and the national press. Applications may be pending for between two and five years. However, priority is afforded once the application is lodged.

The protection arising from registration of a trademark continues for 10 years, after which time the registration may be renewed. Where the mark is not used for a consecutive five-year period without justification, it can be removed from the Register upon application by a third party. In the months following the end of a protection period, the registrar will notify the owner of the mark that protection has now ended. If the owner of a mark fails to submit a request to renew within the following six months from the date of termination of protection, the registrar will delete the mark from the Register.

A trademark owner cannot license the use of a product or service in respect of which there is a registered trademark beyond the period specified for protection of that mark. Forgery of a registered mark is punishable with imprisonment of up to two years or a fine of up to RO2,000.

Unregistered marks also have some protection by virtue of Articles 47 and 48 of the Oman Commercial Law, which protect merchants against deception or fraud or use of a trade name belonging to another owner. These sections allow for injunctive relief as well as compensation.

Illegal competition

Under Royal Decree 38/2000 and Oman Commercial Law, Royal Decree 55/1990, Articles 47–50, there is an overriding principle that it is illegal to engage in competitive business which violates good trade practice, expressed as 'violative of decent practice in industry or trade'. This ban includes:

- business that generates confusion as to the origin, commodity or service when a certain industrial or commercial business is carried out;

- unjustified or unrealistic propaganda against any commercial or industrial product intended to undermine its reputation or fame or confidence in it; and

- use of data or claims while carrying on an industrial or commercial business that misleads people as to the distinguishing features of goods and services.

The precise scope of these illegal competition provisions has yet to be tested.

Trade secrets

Article 34 of Royal Decree 38/2000 has criminalized the disclosure of trade secrets. The Decree gives only limited guidance as to what will be classified as a trade secret, but a view taken (given that it is currently untested in the courts) is that matters will be confidential if their trade value is derived from their secrecy or if reasonable provision has been made to safeguard their secrecy.

Patents

Patents are governed by Royal Decree 82/2000 and the Gulf Cooperation Council (GCC) Patents Regulations.

An invention can be patented if it is new, contains a novel idea, and is worthy of industrial application. However, it must not be inconsistent with public discipline or etiquette, undermine national security or be incompatible with the Islamic Shariah.

The first to apply for a particular invention patent will have priority unless the patent relates to a joint work, in which case (without agreement to the contrary) entitlement to the patent is equal. An applicant who has merely implemented the ideas of others without contributing to the innovation is not entitled to a patent. Employers are treated as the owners of a patent arising out of an employee's work, although the inventor in such a case is entitled to fair remuneration.

Certain 'discoveries' may not be patented. These include scientific and mathematical theories, computer programmes, purely mental activities and games, plant or animal research, biological techniques for the production of plants, animals, plant varieties and animal species, and methods of treating and diagnosing human or animal diseases.

Applications for patents are to be made to the Department of Agencies and Intellectual Property at the Ministry of Commerce and Industry. An application may be withdrawn by the applicant at any stage prior to the Ministry's final decision. If the application is rejected, the applicant has 15 days in which to appeal before this right is lost. An appeal is made to a committee appointed by the Minister of Commerce and Industry. This committee's decision is final. Alternatively, if the patent is awarded, a second interested party may contest the award within 60 days of notification.

The patent owner may use, manufacture, import or offer the product for sale and no third party may exploit the patent without permission of the patent owner. However, a patent offers no protection against innocent infringement carried out prior to a patent's registration. If such infringement were bona fide, the infringer may continue regardless of the registration.

A patent is valid for 20 years from the date on which it is granted. Patents pending are subject to the same protection as if they were fully patented. A patent owner may license his patent contractually or it may be compulsorily licensed if the owner does not exploit a patent for three years, or refuses to contractually license the patent where this obstructs industrial or commercial activity in Oman. A compulsory licence is issued by the minister. Breach of a patent will give rise to both civil and criminal sentences.

In practice, however, it is far more common to have a patent registered at the GCC Patent Office in Riyadh, Saudi Arabia, as this gives the patent-owner protection throughout the GCC. The GCC patent regulations mirror the Omani regulations almost identically.

Copyright

An author's copyright and related rights are protected in Oman under Royal Decree 37/2000. This details the nature of the work and the authors who can enjoy the protections afforded, their rights, and penalties for non-compliance. The protection is afforded to authors of original literary, scientific, technical and cultural works in general, irrespective of their value. Protection is also afforded to translators, persons who summarize, adapt or change the work so as to make it appear in a new form. The rights enjoyed include the author's 'moral' right to have his work ascribed to him or published in a pen name. No omission, change or addition to his work may be made without the author's approval. There is no time limit on these rights.

Financial rights are also afforded. The author has the right to receive royalties for any copying, translation, adaptation, performance or exploitation of his work. Limitations are also imposed, including quoting the work by way of illustration or using the work for educational purposes. Such rights continue for 50 years after the author's death. Infringement of copyright is punishable by imprisonment of up to two years or a fine of no more than RO2,000.

Industrial drawings and patterns

Industrial drawings and patterns are regulated by Royal Decree 39/2000. Only those trade drawings and patterns registered in the Trade Drawings and Patterns Register at the Ministry of Commerce and Industry enjoy protection. The registration of the drawing or pattern is deemed proof of ownership unless the contrary is proved. Ownership vests in the person who created the relevant drawing or design. The design must be original and decent to enjoy protection.

The protection of a registered drawing or pattern lasts for 10 years from the date of submission of application for its registration. It may be renewed for further 10-year periods provided the renewal request is made within the last three months of the protection period. Copying the registered design is punishable by imprisonment or fine and the owner of a design may obtain injunctions preventing third parties from using protected drawings for commercial purposes.

3.2

Practicalities of Intellectual Property

Alaa Edin Mohamed Ahmed, Abu Ghazaleh Intellectual Property, TMP Agents, Muscat

Trademark registration system

The Sultanate of Oman became a member of the Paris Convention for the Protection of Industrial Property on 1 July 1999. International classification of goods and services is followed in Oman, with the exception of Class 33 covering alcohol. Separate application should be filed with respect to each class of goods or services.

The trademark application is examined by the registrar to ensure its availability for registration. The registrar may object in writing to certain aspects of the mark in the course of examination such as the scope of goods or services, or may ask for modification of the mark. Accepted trademarks for registration are published in the *Official Gazette* and in a local daily newspaper. A term of two months from publication in the *Official Gazette* is given for any interested party to oppose the registration of the trademark. In the absence of opposition, the published trademark will mature into the final registration and a final certificate will be issued. Duration of a trademark or service mark registration is 10 years from the filing date, renewable for similar periods of 10 years apiece. A grace period of six months is allowed for filing a renewal application, with a late fine for the same. Renewals should be published in the *Official Gazette* and in a daily newspaper. A trademark that is not renewed may not be registered in the name of others for the same or similar goods or services before the elapse of three years from the cancellation date.

Use of the trademark is not compulsory for filing applications or maintaining the registration in force. However, trademark registration becomes vulnerable to cancellation by any interested party who can establish the fact that the trademark was not actually used for a period of five years in succession, unless the trademark owner presents justification for non-use. Trademarks can be assigned, mortgaged or seized together with the goodwill, unless agreed otherwise. Assignment or mortgage will not have any legal effects towards others unless it is recorded in the Trademark Office Register and published in the *Official Gazette*.

Trademark registration can be licensed to any natural or juridical person to use the mark on all or part of goods or services for which the mark was registered. The owner has the right to license others to use the same mark. The licence period may not exceed the protection period of the trademark. No licence will have any legal effect towards others until after it has been recorded in the Register and the details have been published. The recording of a licence can be cancelled pursuant to an owner's request or after providing proof of the termination or revocation of the licence contract.

The counterfeiting or imitating of registered trademarks in such a manner as to deceive the public; the use of counterfeits or imitated trademarks; the selling, offering for sale, circulating, possessing for the purpose of sale products bearing counterfeit trademarks; and the use with bad intent of a mark identical or similar to a well-known registered or unregistered trademark and which causes confusion to consumers will all be punishable under the law.

Requirements

The requirements for registration of a trade mark in Oman are as follows:

- a power of attorney notarized and duly legalized by an Omani consulate abroad or, in the absence of such a consulate, by a consulate of another Arab country;

- a certified copy of the Articles of Incorporation of the applicant; an extract of the entry in the Commercial Register; or a certificate of good standing for the company;

- a certified copy of the priority document if priority is claimed. A priority document should be submitted to the trademark office within three months of filing the application.

Patent registration system

The Sultanate of Oman is party to the GCC Patent Law, which provides effective protection to member countries of the GCC – namely Bahrain, Kuwait, Oman, Qatar, Saudi Arabia and the United Arab Emirates. In addition, Oman has its own Patent Law, Royal Decree 82/2000, issued in October 2000. However, the implementing regulations of this law have yet to be issued and thus it is not possible to file a patent application according to this law at present. The main features of this law can be summarized as:

The invention may be patented if it is novel, of an inventive step, non-obvious and industrially applicable whether related to novel industrial products or produced by currently used industrial means or by new application of known industrial means. The validity of the patent registration is 20 years from the date of grant. The invention will also be protected from the date of filing the patent application until the date of the patent grant. Patent applications accepted by the Intellectual Property Department have to be published in the manner stipulated by the implementing regulation. Any interested party may, within 60 days, present a written petition to the Department, which has to decide on the petition within 30 days. The patent proprietor may assign the rights of exploiting the patent in part or in its entirety. Such assignment will only be valid after registration and announced as per the conditions and regulations of the law. Any party presenting false or counterfeit documents or information in an attempt to grant a patent for an invention; any party imitating an invention or production method; or any party intentionally infringing any right stipulated by the law will be liable to imprisonment, a fine, or both.

Design and industrial drawing registration system

The Industrial Drawing and Design Law, Royal Decree 39/2000, has recently been issued. The implementing regulations of this law have not yet been issued and thus it is not possible to file any design or industrial drawing application at present. The main features of this law can be summarized as:

As defined by the law, an industrial drawing or design is any arrangement containing lines, colours or any coloured or uncoloured physical shape intended for use in industrial production whether mechanically or manually and including textile designs, provided that this arrangement or design gives a special appearance to the industrial or handicraft product.

The validity of the design registration is 10 years from the filing date, renewable for a further term of the same. Any action concerning the assignment of ownership or the licence of industrial drawings or designs will not have any effect unless this action is recorded in the relevant register. Imitation of industrial drawings or designs protected under the law; knowingly offering them for sale or circulation; possessing them for the purpose of selling products containing them; or imitating them in any way will all be punishable under the law.

Copyright registration system

Oman has been party to the Berne Convention since July 1999. The Law for the Protection of Copyright and Neighbouring Rights, Royal Decree 37/2000, governs the protection of copyright and neighbouring rights in Oman. However, the implementing regulations have yet to be issued. The main features of the law can be summarized as:

The law grants protection to authors of literary, artistic and scientific works whatever the value, kind, purpose or way of expression of the work. In general, the protection will be provided for those works whose means of expression include writing, sound, drawing, image production or motion picture. It also includes creative titles and computer software. Financial rights are granted to an author during his lifetime and for 50 calendar years commencing from the beginning of the first calendar year following his death; and for 50 years from the date of the first publication of movies, applied artworks and photographs, works published under a pseudonym or without mentioning the author's name, and works published for the first time posthumously.

Requirements

The requirements for registration of copyright in Oman are:

- a power of attorney legalized by an Omani consulate;
- three original samples of the work;
- three copies of the work;
- a copy of the home-country registration certificate or of a registration effective elsewhere.

3.3

Privatization Initiatives

Sridhar Sridharan, Tax Partner, Ernst & Young, Muscat

Introduction

Privatization has become an important feature of Omani economic development. Driven forward by the government, numerous projects across many sectors of the economy have already been progressed by or in association with the private sector, both domestic and international, and more are expected to follow in the future. This chapter provides an insight into current thinking on privatization and the progress made to date, while also alluding to future intentions in this regard.

The power sector

The Omani government has unveiled its plans to privatize the power sector. The plan involves the unbundling and corporatization of the existing activities into a number of generation, transmission and distribution businesses. The new companies, to be owned initially by the government, will be privatized in due course. A new law will be drafted to set up a specialized regulatory body to monitor the privatized power companies.

Developments relating to the privatization of three major power projects

Barka power and desalination project

The US$450 million Barka power and desalination project was awarded to AES Corporation of the United States in November 2000. The project, which is to generate 427 megawatts of power and produce 3,800 cubic metres of water per hour, is scheduled for start-up in April 2003. Enel Power of Italy and Hitachi Zosen Corporation of Japan are the EPC (Engineering, Procurement and Construction) contractors.

Al Kamil power project

A build-own-operate contract for 15 years for the 275-megawatt power project in the Sharqiyah region (Al Kamil) has been awarded to International Power of the United Kingdom.

This project involves the design, financing, construction, commissioning, ownership, operation and maintenance of a single-cycle power station in the province (wilayat) of Al Kamil in Al Sharqiyah region. The station will utilize natural gas to produce 275 megawatts of electric power to substitute the existing diesel-operated power stations in the provinces of Al Sharqiyah region.

The project will sell power to the government under a 15-year purchase agreement, with commercial operation having commenced in April 2002.

Salalah power project

The government has signed a Memorandum of Understanding with the Dhofar Power Consortium (DPC) in connection with the privatization of the Salalah power system. PSEG Global, a US multinational, is the leader of the DPC. The Salalah power system is a vertically integrated utility involving power generation, transmission, distribution and billing and is the first of its kind in the Middle East. The initial investment of the project is expected to amount to US$260 million. India's Larsen & Toubro is the EPC contractor.

Wastewater treatment projects

Muscat wastewater project

The negotiations between the government and a consortium, headed by Galfar Engineering & Contracting of Oman, for the past few years for the Muscat Waste Water project have ceased. The government is yet to decide whether to implement the project through the public or private sector.

Salalah wastewater commercialization

The Ministry of National Economy has appointed a consortium – including Ernst & Young as lead and financial adviser, Curtis-Mallet-Provost as legal adviser and Mott MacDonald as technical adviser – to provide advisory services on the commercialization of the government-owned company responsible for developing and operating the Salalah wastewater project. The project will provide sewerage and wastewater treatment facilities to Salalah, the capital of the southern Dhofar region. The construction phase has been undertaken entirely by the Omani government. The facilities will ultimately be privatized in line with the government's privatization programme. The objective of the commercialization phase is to encourage the company to act as a commercially viable entity, which will permit private-sector participation to be introduced at a later stage.

Airports

In a move to attract private investment in infrastructure projects, the government has taken measures to privatize the airports. Credit Suisse First Boston (CSFB) was appointed as financial consultants for conducting a feasibility study for the project. The government announced in early December 2000 the commencement of the tender process to select a strategic partner to manage its two main airports at Seeb and Salalah. The government's main objective is to introduce international airport management and expertise to improve the competitive position, route network and efficiency of airports. The strategic partner is expected to be able to demonstrate the skills and be committed to the development of a new terminal at Muscat at the earliest feasible opportunity. A consortium comprising the British Airports Authority (BAA), Asea Brown Boveri (ABB) and Sheikh Suhail Bahwan was chosen late in 2001 as the strategic partner.

Telecommunications

The government took the first step towards privatizing the telecommunications sector in 1999 by transforming the General Telecommunications Organization (GTO) into an Omani closed joint-stock company (SAOC). The new company, Oman Telecommunications Company (OmanTel), is fully owned by the government. The move to privatize GTO paves the way for expanded participation of the private sector in government-sponsored projects. The minister of telecommunications has announced that the government is in the final stages of preparation for inviting strategic investors to purchase a stake in OmanTel. The government also intends to offer part of OmanTel to the public.

Roads

The Ministry of Housing, Electricity and Water intends to allow investors to construct new roads that will be subject to toll under a system of privatization. The investors will build, operate and transfer the roads to the ministry after a specified period. Feasibility studies have already been made in preparation for the privatization of the Al Batinah highway and Sur-Qurayyat coastal road.

Sohar port

The Ministry of Housing, Electricity and Water has announced its plans for the privatization of Sohar port in due course.

Industrial estates

The director-general of industry at the Ministry of Commerce and Industry confirmed in April 2000 that the Ministry had conducted a study with a view to privatizing or transforming the country's industrial estates into public companies.

Tourism-related initiatives

The Ministry of Commerce and Industry is currently producing a tourism strategy to develop and expand the Sultanate's tourism sector. The sector's contribution to GDP is expected to reach 18 per cent in 2020. The Majlis Ash'Shura (Consultative Council) discussed and approved a draft Tourism Law after making certain amendments. The approved draft was then referred to the Council of Ministers.

Privatization: related legal changes

In awarding the three privatization projects relating to the power sector, the government has superseded certain provisions of the Privatization Law issued in 1996 and the Commercial Companies Law (CCL) issued in 1974.

Part 4

The Fiscal and Regulatory Framework

4.1

Financial Reporting and Auditing

Philip Stanton, Managing Partner, Ernst & Young, Muscat

Statutory requirements

Required books and records

Oman's Commercial Law requires all business enterprises to maintain the following books at a minimum:

- a day book maintaining a daily record of all activities related to the commercial enterprise;

- a monthly record of personal withdrawals (for proprietorships and partnerships);

- a stock book listing inventory, by quantity and by value, held at year end.

Under the law, the Ministry of Commerce and Industry must attest to the records listed above. However, this requirement is temporarily suspended. The secretary-general for taxation (SGT) has the right to inspect accounting records.

Accounting records must be maintained in Omani Rials unless the taxpayer obtains permission from the Ministry of Finance to use a foreign currency. Accounting records may be maintained in Arabic or other languages.

Method of accounting

Enterprises must use the accrual method of accounting unless the SGT has granted approval to use another method.

Financial statements

Companies with capital exceeding RO20,000 (US$52,000) must submit audited financial statements and other information with their final tax declaration. The minimum capital requirement applies to the capital of the entire company, and not simply to the capital of the foreign branch. Filed financial statements must be prepared in Arabic.

Sources of accounting principles and practices

Omani law requires enterprises to follow International Accounting Standards (IAS). Otherwise, principles and practices of accounting are not codified.

Financial reporting

Joint-stock companies must prepare audited financial statements within three months following their year end and provide their shareholders with audited balance sheets and profit and loss statements 21 days before the annual shareholders' meeting.

If a limited liability company (LLC) appoints an auditor, the LLC must prepare audited financial statements and provide its shareholders with audited balance sheets and profit and loss statements within six months after its year end.

Banks must file their audited financial statements with the Central Bank of Oman within three months after their year end. Insurance companies must file their audited financial statements with the commissioner of insurance at the Ministry of Commerce and Industry within five months after their year end. Companies listed on the Muscat Securities Market (MSM) are required to publish non-audited financial information on a quarterly basis and should comply with certain disclosure standards.

Muscat Securities Market (MSM)

The Muscat Securities Market (MSM), which began operations in 1989, oversees the flow of funds into securities and develops the local financial market. The capitalization of the market and the number of companies listed on it are growing. In December 1999, the value of listed shares was more than RO2.262 billion (US$5.883 billion); in January 2000, 213 companies were listed.

Membership of the exchange is compulsory for Omani-licensed banks, specialized loan institutions, authorized financial intermediaries, joint-stock companies and Omani public authorities whose shares are registered on the securities market.

Regulations issued in 1998 established a Capital Market Authority (CMA), a depository and a stock exchange.

Audit requirements

Joint-stock companies, as well as LLCs that have more than 10 shareholders or capital exceeding RO50,000 (US$130,000), are required to have annual statutory audits. Other LLCs must have statutory audits if required by their articles of association or if requested by shareholders holding at least 20 per cent of the capital of the company. In addition, companies with capital exceeding RO20,000 (US$52,000) must file audited financial statements with their tax returns.

Accounting profession

The Law Regulating the Accountancy and Auditing Profession sets forth conditions of registration, qualifications and other requirements for accountants and auditors. By June 2001, accounting and audit firms doing business in Oman had to have at least one Omani partner with a minimum capital participation of 35 per cent.

Omani law requires that audits be performed by authorized auditors. A list of authorized auditors is prepared by the Ministry of Commerce and Industry and includes all firms that are registered to operate in Oman. Auditors must be independent of the company being audited and may not provide technical, administrative or consulting services to the company on a regular basis.

4.2

Legal Environment

Sean Angle and Brian Howard, Trowers & Hamlins, Muscat

Constitutional background

The Sultanate of Oman is an absolute monarchy and all the powers of government in Oman vest absolutely in or devolve from the Sultan, who rules with the assistance of an appointed Council of Ministers. Oman has no formal constitution – rather, an administrative structure of the government is formed in accordance with royal decrees issued by the Sultan. Consequently, all legislation and other acts undertaken by the government are subject to his absolute prerogative and the validity of all acts of government officials other than the Sultan is dependent upon the terms of the relevant royal decrees, decisions and regulations.

Pursuant to such royal decrees, ministerial decisions and other regulations are issued from time to time by the ministries and other agencies of the Omani government. All primary and subordinate legislation is published in the *Official Gazette*. Ministerial decisions and regulations are in the most part also published in the *Official Gazette*, although there are certain such decisions and regulations which occasionally remain unpublished. In addition to the laws of Oman as published in the *Official Gazette*, Oman also applies a system of Shariah law, which has, however, only limited application to commercial matters, dealing principally with matters of family law.

Basic Law of the State

The Basic Law of the State (promulgated by Royal Decree 101/1996) provides for the system of governance in Oman and states, in Article 2, that 'Islam is the religion of the State and the Islamic Shariah is the basis of legislation'. It also states, in Article 77, that existing laws and regulations remain in force 'provided that they do not conflict with any of the provisions of this Basic Law'.

The Basic Law establishes certain fundamental rights of nationals and expatriates including the protection of personal liberty and property interests. The Basic Law also deals with how the issue of succession is handled, the duties of the Sultan, ownership of the country's natural resources, the fundamental rights of citizens and the basic economic, social and political principles upon which the government is based.

The Basic Law provides for the establishment of a court with jurisdiction to determine whether legislation complies with the provisions of the Basic Law. Royal Decree 90/1999 envisages the establishment of a judicial body within the Supreme Court, which will have such powers. However, the Supreme Court is a new beast to Oman and it is as yet to be seen how it will discharge its functions.

Matters of a commercial nature are largely dealt with outside the Shariah unless both parties agree that it shall apply. Currently, the Commercial Division of the Court of First Instance and the Courts of Summary Jurisdiction are the only bodies in Oman with jurisdiction in relation to commercial disputes. However, the above-mentioned Royal Decree 90/1999 provides for a completely overhauled court system and sets out the different levels of courts as follows:

1. Supreme Court.

2. Appellate Courts.

3. Courts of First Instance.

4. Courts of Summary Jurisdiction.

These courts are competent to hear civil and commercial matters, labour, tax and rent cases, in addition to arbitration applications. In addition, Royal Decree 91/1999 provided for the establishment of the Administrative Court, which is an independent judicial body with exclusive powers to review decisions issued by government bodies. The Administrative Court has the power to award compensation to persons aggrieved by government bodies. Inactivity of a government body is now caught within this court's jurisdiction and is sufficient to ground an action if the complainant has exhausted all internal appeal processes.

As in all modern legal systems, the judges are under a duty to remain impartial. There is a mechanism in place whereby the performance of judges is reviewed periodically, as is the hearing of complaints against judges.

Basis of the legal system

Much of the legislation in Oman is consistent with that in force in other Gulf Cooperation Council (GCC) countries. Omani law shows a considerable degree of Egyptian influence, which in turn has clear derivations from a 'French'-based or, more generally, 'civil law' influence. There are also particular areas of legislation in Oman that show clear 'common law' influence, of which the Banking Law is probably the most important example. It is notable that modern Omani judges are still influenced by reference to Egyptian legislation and cases.

Procedure for implementation of a new law

There is no fixed procedure for promoting a new decree, save to the extent that a decree needs to be sponsored by a ministry or other government body and is subject to review by the Ministry of Legal Affairs.

Oman has an *Official Gazette*, which is used as the means of publishing new legislation, including delegated legislation. The date of implementation of legislation is generally the date of issue of the *Gazette* in which the legislation is published. The effective date of new legislation will nearly always be specified and it is unusual for legislation to come into effect more than a few months after the date of the relevant *Gazette* issue. Implementing legislation can take some time to put in place and this can lead to difficulties in applying legislation that is already in force.

Specific legal principles

Freedom of contract

Under Omani law, the parties to a contract, particularly a commercial contract, are largely free to arrange their own affairs subject to mandatory legislative provisions. However, the concept of 'that which is not prohibited is permitted' has not been developed as a formal legal doctrine. Freedom of contract depends upon the precedence given by the courts to contractual terms and will therefore be subject to mandatory rules of law and public policy as understood and applied by the courts.

Conflict of contractual provisions with public policy or order

Contractual provisions that contradict express statutory provisions in Oman will not be upheld. As an example, under the Commercial Agencies Law, an agent is entitled to compensation should the agency agreement be terminated without justification, notwithstanding that due notice may have been given in accordance with the terms of the contract.

Statutory limitation periods

Article 92 of the Commercial Code establishes a limitation period of 10 years for commercial obligations generally. This general rule is subject to specific periods relating to matters such as the carriage of goods (one year) other than bill of lading claims (two years), agency relationships (three years from the expiry of the agency agreement) and banking law claims. A five-year limitation period applies to claims against the government. Claims by the government are subject to a seven-year limitation period.

Negligence

There is no developed concept of negligence under Omani law. However, it is likely that, where the actions of one party have caused damage to another, a compensation claim could be advanced.

Recent soundings from the courts indicate that, where an action of a third party had caused damage to the plaintiff, the plaintiff is entitled to compensation if the following three elements are satisfied: fault, damage and a causal relationship between the fault and the damage.

Choice of governing law clauses in contracts

Omani law does not impose any limitation or restriction in relation to choice of governing law clauses in contracts, provided that such choice is not contrary to public order. However, the courts have stated that they would not feel able to apply a chosen foreign law unless the parties to a case before it are able to bring evidence, and to agree upon that evidence, as to the chosen foreign law. The author is aware of only one case in which the court has in fact applied a law other than the law of Oman and this decision was not based on a Choice of Governing Law Clause (Appeal Case No. 45/1998, Judicial Yearbook 98/99 p258, Date of Judgement 14.12.98). The choice of a foreign law is more likely to be successful in the context of an arbitration.

4.3

Legal Dispute and Arbitration Procedures

*James Harbridge and Brian Howard,
Trowers & Hamlins, Muscat*

As with all things in Oman, arbitration procedures and systems are relatively new given that the modern Sultanate and its legal system have only been in existence since 1970. Consequently, the law and judicial system has been subject to movement as Oman tries to establish the best approach for its people by drawing from other states' international experience and its ever-significant heritage. It is therefore unlikely that this chapter will constitute the final word on the judicial system and up-to-date advice should always be sought when entering Oman's dispute resolution arena.

Courts of justice

The courts that exist in Oman are the Courts of First Instance (divided into the Criminal Division, the Civil Division (consisting of the Summary Justice and First Instance tiers) and the Shariah Division), the Appeal Court and the Supreme Court. There is also an Administrative Court.

The Summary Justice tier was established in 1997 and settles claims of up to RO15,000. A decision of the Summary Justice tier may be appealed to the Civil Division First Instance tier where the amount claimed exceeds RO5,000.

A Judgement of the Civil Division First Instance tier may be appealed to the Appeal Court where the amount claimed exceeds RO25,000.

In addition, the Administrative Court became operational in April 2001. This new court is designed to provide a forum for a review of decisions made by government bodies. The court (which comprises First Instance and Appeal circuits) has the power to reverse decisions made by government bodies and can also award compensation.

The Supreme Court will soon be in session. Put simply, it will act, in certain circumstances which may be detailed in the pending civil and commercial procedure law, as a third layer of justice where parties wish to challenge judgements made by the Appeal Courts.

Arbitration

Where contracts contain an arbitration clause, the Commercial Court would normally uphold the requirement to arbitrate, and would not usually hear the merits of a case in respect of a contract where an arbitration clause was included. The Oman Arbitration Law, Royal Decree 47/1997, governs private arbitrations in Oman and provides a framework for such arbitrations, which is based on the Egyptian version of the UNCITRAL model law.

Principle of precedent

There is no formal principle of precedent in Oman and the courts have indicated that they do not consider themselves bound by their previous decisions. Nevertheless, the courts, if directed to previous decisions, are likely to take note of those decisions. This practice arises from the need for consistency in judicial decision-making but is limited by a legal tradition which reasons from general principles of law and treats each case on its own merits. Royal Decree 90/1999 provides that judgements of the Supreme Court shall only deviate from legal precedents set by previous Supreme Court judgements where the amending decision is made by a court comprising the president or vice-president and 10 of the most senior judges. Although this may only take place at the very highest level, it will be interesting to see whether this will lead to the development of a system of precedent akin to that found in common law jurisdictions.

In issuing their judgements, the courts adhere to the royal decrees and laws in force in the Sultanate, contracts between the disputing parties (provided that the conditions of such contracts do not conflict with any law, public order or propriety or established valid practices in the field of commercial activities) and whatever establishes justice between the litigants and leads to the stabilization of commercial transactions.

Oman has a Commercial Code, Royal Decree 55/1990, as amended, which provides that the Commercial Court should consider the following matters in interpreting commercial contracts:

- the terms of the contract;

- legislative provisions;
- rules of custom and practice;
- the Islamic Shariah.

It is noted that the factors listed above are generally applied by the courts in descending order of priority. With respect to the application of rules of custom, the Commercial Code gives precedence to 'local' over 'general' custom.

Oman does not have a Civil Code, and judges frequently rely on principles derived from the Civil Code of Egypt where Omani law and local custom leave room for ambiguity in relation to a specific issue.

Remedies

Remedies in Oman are discretionary. There is no guarantee that specific performance or other equitable remedies will be granted by the courts, although the courts are competent to grant these remedies. Precautionary remedies are often difficult to obtain. The applicant must satisfy the court that there is an 'immediate threat' to the interests of the applicant. The Commercial Division of the Court of First Instance almost invariably makes awards of damages.

Legal costs

Legal costs generally are not recoverable in litigation in Oman. However, the court may order the losing party to pay the filing fees and the fees of any court-appointed expert. The court may not uphold a contractual right to recover legal costs. In an arbitration process, it can be agreed between parties that legal costs will be recoverable.

Court hearings

All court proceedings take place in Arabic. Accordingly, documents originally prepared in another language must be translated into Arabic before presentation to a court. Such a process can result in difficulties due to differences between the original-language version and the Arabic translation. It can, however, be agreed between the parties to an arbitration that proceedings be conducted in English.

Appellate system

A judgement is capable of appeal if it is in respect of a sum which exceeds RO25,000, unless it is a matter that has been assigned to and heard by one of the Summary Courts (in which case an appeal is possible to the Court of First Instance if the judgement is in respect of a claim in excess of RO5,000). Filing of an appeal must take place within 30 days of the date of judgement, or within 30 days of the date upon which the prospective appellant was notified of the written judgement if the party had not been present when judgement was delivered. A judgement may not be enforced until the time for lodging an appeal has expired and, if an appeal is lodged, until the determination of the appeal.

Enforcement of an arbitration award or court judgement obtained against an Omani company

Enforcement of judgements obtained before the Omani courts, or of arbitration awards where the arbitration was conducted before the courts, or of a private arbitration award obtained in Oman, is undertaken by the Court of First Instance Civil Division, to whom application for enforcement must be made. The assets of the Omani party against which enforcement is requested must be identified in the application. Notice will be given to the judgement debtor. Seven days thereafter enforcement may take place against those assets by seizure, following which they will be sold at auction by the court within three months of the date of application for seizure unless otherwise agreed or ordered.

Any party with the benefit of a judgement against the judgement debtor may join in the process of enforcement.

A judgement may be enforced against funds held by any third party due to the company and enforcement may also take place against land, which is generally sold by the court.

The threat of bankruptcy may be relied upon in enforcement proceedings, although it is not necessarily in the interest of a judgement creditor to seek the bankruptcy of the judgement debtor as all other established creditors will prove in any recovery.

Reference by the courts of Oman to decisions of the courts of other states

It is open to any litigant to make reference to decisions of courts of another state, whether Arab or otherwise. The court may or may not take note of these decisions at its discretion.

Choice of jurisdiction

Submission by a company to the jurisdiction of the courts of a state other than Oman should be binding if so expressed, although the courts may nevertheless accept jurisdiction on the basis that its jurisdiction is established by royal decree.

Recognition of a foreign judgement

Prior to the introduction of Royal Decree 13/1997, there were no formal rules for recognition of foreign judgements or arbitration awards, and the parties could be required to re-litigate the matter in Oman. There are now express reciprocal enforcement provisions that may be applied by the Omani courts. These are subject to a number of conditions being fulfilled, including that both parties (or their representatives) must appear before the courts, that the judgement must not be contrary to Omani law and must have been obtained in a jurisdiction in which Omani judgements or arbitration awards are enforceable. This potential for formal recognition of a foreign judgement or arbitral award is of considerable importance. Consequently, Oman's ratification of the Convention on the Enforcement of Judgement Disputes and Judicial Summons in the Arab Gulf Cooperative Council States and the 1958 New York Convention on the Recognition and Enforcement of Foreign Arbitral Awards were important steps forward.

Oman is a signatory to the Convention on the Settlement of Investment Disputes between States and Nationals of Other States (the ICSID Convention) and has entered into a number of investment protection treaties with other states such as the United Kingdom (ratified in Oman by Royal Decree 73/1995) and France (ratified by Royal Decree 74/1995).

Taxation

Sridhar Sridharan, Tax Partner,
Ernst & Young, Muscat

Principal taxes

Introduction

The Omani government imposes tax on the following entities:

- joint-stock companies;
- holding companies;
- limited liability companies (LLCs);
- general and limited partnerships;
- joint ventures;
- branches of foreign companies.

In addition, the following individuals are treated as taxable entities:

- non-Omani individuals carrying out revenue-generating business activities;
- Omani sole proprietors.

Citizens of other Gulf Cooperation Council (GCC) countries are treated as Omani residents for tax purposes if they are engaged in specified economic activities and if certain conditions are met. Details of these economic activities are:

Oman's restrictions on foreign ownership do not apply to GCC nationals investing in or pursuing activities in certain areas, including industry, agriculture, animal husbandry, fishing, construction, hotel and catering business, retail and wholesale trade, operation and maintenance of hospitals, and education. Oman has specified certain conditions that must be met for GCC nationals to invest in and pursue activities in these areas.

Direct and indirect taxes

Direct taxes in Oman comprise income tax imposed on companies and trading and industrial establishments and certain municipal taxes. No personal income tax is assessed in the Sultanate.

Customs duty is the only indirect tax imposed in Oman.

Customs duties

Most imported goods are subject to customs duty levied at a flat rate of 5 per cent on their cost-insurance-freight (CIF) value. Consumer goods, including foodstuffs, are exempt from customs duty. Alcohol and tobacco are subject to higher rates of duty. Goods produced within the GCC generally may be imported duty-free. In certain circumstances, Oman may permit contractors to import duty-free equipment and materials for use on government, Petroleum Development Oman (PDO) and Oman LNG (OLNG) projects. Oman may impose higher rates of customs duty on the import of goods that compete with locally produced goods.

Oman does not impose quotas or other non-tariff trade barriers, has not enacted antidumping regulations and does not impose export duties.

Sources of tax law

The Income Tax Decree of 1971 introduced taxation in Oman. This decree was superseded by the Law of Income Tax on Companies, Royal Decree 47/1981. The Law of Profit Tax on Commercial and Industrial Establishments, Royal Decree 77/1989, published on 16 September 1989, introduced a tax on business establishments that are wholly owned by Omani citizens. However, subsequent decrees exempted these businesses from the tax until 31 December 1993. The Law of Profit Tax also introduced a tax on commercial and industrial establishments that are owned or operated by non-Omani individuals.

All tax legislation is enacted by royal decree and all provisions implementing tax laws are introduced by ministerial decisions.

Tax administration

Registration

Establishments may register with the tax authorities by filing a declaration form specifying certain business information. A foreign establishment may register with the office of the secretary-general for taxation (SGT), which is a department of the Ministry of Finance, even if the establishment has not formally registered with the Ministry of Commerce and Industry.

Filing and payment

Taxpayers must use a 12-month period to prepare their financial statements for tax purposes and, in general, use the calendar year. For a first accounting period, the taxpayer may elect to use a period of up to 18 months.

Legally, all tax returns must be prepared in Arabic, although in practice returns prepared in English are also accepted. Provisional income tax returns must be filed within three months after the end of the accounting period. The return must state the taxpayer's estimated taxable income and must be accompanied by payment for the amount of tax due. Annual income tax returns must be filed within six months after the end of the accounting period. If any tax is due (the tax liability exceeding the amount of tax paid with the provisional return), payment for the excess amount must be submitted with the annual return. Delayed payment of taxes is subject to a penalty at a monthly rate of 1 per cent of the amount of tax overdue. Tax overpayments may be carried forward, may be refunded or may be offset against tax owed, but only if the overpayment is determined by an assessment.

Certain companies must submit audited financial statements and other information with their final tax declarations.

Financial statements

Companies with capital exceeding RO20,000 (US$52,000) must submit audited financial statements and other information with their final tax declaration. The minimum capital requirement applies to the capital of the entire company, and not simply to the capital of the foreign branch. Filed financial statements must be prepared in Arabic.

Audit requirements

Joint-stock companies, in addition to limited liability companies (LLCs) with more than 10 shareholders or capital exceeding RO50,000 (US$130,000), are required to have annual statutory audits. Other LLCs must have statutory audits if required by their articles of association or if requested by shareholders holding at least 20 per cent of the capital of the company. In addition, companies with capital exceeding RO20,000 (US$52,000) must file audited financial statements with their tax returns.

Assessments and appeals

If a taxpayer fails to file the required tax declarations or conceals income, the SGT may make arbitrary assessments at any time. If declarations are filed, assessments must be made within five years after the year in which the declaration is filed.

Taxpayers may appeal an assessment at four levels. Those contesting assessments may present their arguments to the SGT and any decision of that office may be appealed to a committee designated by the Ministry of Finance. Appeals of these decisions may subsequently be made to the Primary Court and finally to the Appeals Court.

Penalties

In addition to the penalty for late payments of tax, the Tax Law imposes penalties for tax evasion and for other failures to comply with the law.

Tax inspection field audits

Currently, tax inspection field audits are not conducted. The Tax Law requires taxpayers to maintain accounting books and records for 10 years after the end of the accounting period to which the books and records relate.

Resident corporations

Tax rates

Companies are taxed at progressive rates – for details of these, see Appendix A to this chapter.

Special tax provisions apply to petroleum companies. In general, companies deriving income from the sale of petroleum are taxed on their taxable income derived from such sales at a rate of 55 per cent, subject to certain conditions. However, the tax provisions contained in the concession (production-sharing) agreement generally override the tax rules. Such agreements specify the method of computing taxable income and obligate the government to settle the concessionaire's tax liability.

Territoriality

Companies conducting business in Oman are subject to tax on Omani source income. Foreign entities are subject to tax if they have a 'permanent establishment' in Oman. The term 'permanent establishment' is widely interpreted, but generally means a fixed place of business where an establishment carries on all or part of its business.

Determination of taxable income

Taxable income is the net profit reported in the audited financial statements, adjusted for tax purposes. It includes gross income less deductions that are generally incurred by a commercial enterprise.

Gross income

Tax is assessed on income that is realized or arises in Oman, or that is deemed to be realized or arising in Oman by the SGT. Income includes business profits, interest, royalties and that arising from other sources.

International Accounting Standards (IAS) and generally accepted methods of commercial accounting must be followed. The accrual method must be used to determine income, unless the SGT permits the taxpayer to use a different method – for example, the cash or modified accrual method.

Dividends

Dividends are not taxed.

Capital gains

Capital gains derived from the sale of fixed assets and acquired intangible assets are taxed at the same rates as ordinary income. Capital gains are not granted special treatment for tax purposes.

Compensation for services

Income for services rendered in Oman is subject to tax if the recipient has a permanent establishment in Oman, regardless of whether the payments are received outside Oman.

Supply and turnkey contracts

No tax is imposed on profits derived from a supply contract that terminates before or upon reaching an Omani port if the supplier has no activity within Oman.

Taxpayers must report the full amount of income received under turnkey (supply and installation) contracts. Turnkey contracts generally involve the following distinct phases:

- design;
- supply;
- installation;
- supervision;
- commission.

The first two phases, design and supply, are generally performed offshore; however, if these two phases are determined to be the subject matter of a single contract, income attributed to these two phases is included in Omani taxable income.

Interest

If an LLC advances funds to a shareholder or other related party interest-free or at a below-market rate, the tax authorities may deem that the company earned interest income on the advancement of funds.

Long-term contracts

The percentage-of-completion method must be used to account for long-term contracts.

Foreign source income

No provisions exist for taxing foreign source income. However, Omani companies with foreign branches are taxed on that income.

Valuation of assets

Fixed assets

Fixed assets must be valued at cost. Revaluations are ignored for tax purposes.

Inventory

The Tax Law does not stipulate a required method of accounting for inventories. In general, inventories are valued at the lower of cost and net realizable value, with cost determined using the weighted-average or first in, first out (FIFO) method. Any provisions made in the financial statements to lower the value to net realizable value may not be deducted in computing an entity's taxable income.

Deductions

In general, commercial deductions are allowed for tax purposes.

Depreciation and amortization

Depreciation must be calculated in accordance with the rates listed in Appendix B. Certain start-up costs may be amortized over a three- to five-year period.

Bad debts

Doubtful debts may be deducted only to the extent that the SGT considers them bad and therefore irrecoverable. The taxpayer must demonstrate that it has taken all possible steps to recover the debt, and that the debt is, in fact, a bad rather than doubtful debt.

Reserves

Reserves are generally not deductible.

Provisions

Provisions are generally not deductible, including provisions made for the following:

- Doubtful debts (see Bad debts, above).

- Maintenance.

- Future losses for contractors.

- Obsolete and slow-moving inventory.

However, insurance companies may deduct unexpired risk reserves (technical provisions based on net premiums). In addition, bank loan loss provisions are deductible if approved by the Central Bank of Oman.
Disallowed items are allowed when the expense is actually incurred.

Donations

Donations may be deducted, up to 5 per cent of gross income, only if made to organizations identified by the Council for Financial Affairs.

Insurance agent fees

Under certain circumstances, insurance agent fees paid by branches of foreign insurance companies are deductible up to 25 per cent of the net premium amount.

Interest expense

Interest paid to affiliates of shareholders is generally not deductible, particularly if the tax authorities believe that the borrowing company is under-capitalized.

Tax representation fees

Tax representation fees paid to professional advisers are not deductible for tax purposes because the expense is not incurred for the purpose of generating revenue.

Remuneration to directors, shareholders and partners

In general, remuneration paid to directors, shareholders and partners is deductible for tax purposes, subject to certain conditions.

Rental costs

Rental costs are deductible only if the rental agreements are registered with the government authority.

Tax incentives

Tax exemptions may be available for companies engaged in certain activities.

The Organization and Encouragement of Industry Law, Royal Decree 1/1979, governs the provision of incentives to foreign investors in Oman. The law established the Industrial Development Committee, which seeks to promote increased productivity and efficiency, as well as the development and consolidation of industrial installations. Proposals qualify for incentives only if Omani nationals make up 25 per cent of their total workforce, unless the Ministry of Commerce and Industry specifically rules otherwise.

Investment incentives include the provision of industrial plots in industrial zones for nominal charges (see Industrial zones, below); preference in the allocation of government land; interest-free or subsidized loans with long terms for repayment; reduced charges for water, electricity and fuel; financial assistance for the development of economic and technical feasibility studies; and the expedited arrangement of immigration visas and permits for foreign workers.

Tax exemptions

Tax exemptions from corporate tax and customs duty may be granted by the Ministry of Finance. Tax exemptions are available for entities engaging in manufacturing, mining, agriculture, fishing, fish processing, animal husbandry, tourism, the export of manufactured and reprocessed products, higher education and public utilities. Exemptions are granted for five-year periods effective from the date when production begins or services are first rendered; a five-year extension may be granted. Management agreements and construction contracts do not qualify for tax exemptions.

Companies engaged in the activities listed above may also obtain an exemption from the payment of customs duty on imports of equipment, spare parts and raw materials.

Industrial zones

The Ministry of Commerce and Industry has created industrial zones at Raysut, Rusayl, Sohar and Nizwa. The Ministry plans to establish additional industrial zones at Buraimi, Khasab and Sur. The industrial zones have fully developed plots with appropriate infrastructure facilities. Investment incentives include the provision of industrial plots in industrial zones for nominal charges.

Free Trade Zone

Oman has established a Free Trade Zone located along the borders between Oman and the Republic of Yemen. The zone is located in the town of Al Mazyouna, 260 kilometres from Salalah. The Al Mazyouna zone is managed by the Public Establishment for Industrial Estates (PEIE) and comprises 23 stores, in addition to plots prepared for building new shops, showrooms, warehouses and small manufacturing units. The zone enjoys several privileges and facilities, including transit trade, which permits the flow of commodities free of tax or customs duty across the Omani and Yemeni borders. Commodities may be located in the zone prior to their import into the consuming country.

A Free Trade Zone is under consideration for establishment in Salalah.

Foreign tax relief

The tax authorities may allow relief for foreign taxes paid on a case-by-case basis.

Loss carryovers

Losses may be carried forward for five years but may not be carried back. Net losses incurred by companies benefiting from tax holidays may be carried forward without any time limit under certain circumstances.

Treatment of groups of companies

Omani tax law does not contain specific rules for the taxation of groups of companies under common ownership. Each company within a group is taxed as an independent entity.

Omani tax law addresses the possibility that related parties may seek to avoid or reduce taxation on certain transactions. The SGT may re-characterize a transaction if it determines that an avoidance or reduction of tax has occurred. Deductions of amounts paid to related parties are scrutinized, and a portion of these amounts may be added back to net income.

Dividends, interest and royalties paid to foreign affiliates

Oman does not impose withholding tax on dividends and interest paid to foreign affiliates. Royalties are subject to withholding tax at a rate of 10 per cent.

Non-resident corporations

Omani tax law does not distinguish between resident and non-resident companies. If a company derives income from Oman that involves only occasional visits to the country, this income is taxable. If the payer is an entity taxable in Oman, transactions may be identified through the tax authorities' examination of the payer's file.

Income from subsidiaries

An Omani subsidiary of a foreign-owned company is taxed according to progressive rates that vary according to the level of Omani and foreign participation. For a listing of these rates, see Appendix A.

Branches of foreign companies

Branches of foreign companies are taxed at a single tax rate that varies depending on the entire amount of the branch's taxable income. The applicable tax rate applies to the branch's total taxable income. For a table of these rates, see Appendix A.

For a sample tax calculation for a branch of a foreign company, see Appendix C.

Deductions for branches of foreign companies

The deductibility of expenses incurred by branches of foreign companies is subject to certain limitations, as summarized below.

Head office charges
Ministerial Decision 91/1984 addresses an Omani branch's ability to deduct expenses that are incurred by its head office but cannot be directly attributed to the Omani branch from the books of account and other records. These expenses may be deducted at the lowest of the following amounts:

- expenses allocated by the head office;

- average amount of these expenses, as approved by the SGT during the prior three years;

- 3 per cent of the total income of the branch (5 per cent of the total income for branches of foreign banks and insurance companies (the total income of insurance companies for this purpose is total premiums net of reinsurance) and 10 per cent of the total income for branches of major industrial companies in highly technical fields).

Sponsorship fees
Sponsorship fees paid by branches of foreign companies to Omani agents are deductible up to 5 per cent of taxable income. No deduction is allowed if a loss is reported.

Interest
Interest paid to a head office is disallowed, whether it is paid on a current account balance or is a portion of head office interest costs.

If the Omani branch of a foreign company is funded by a head office current account bearing no interest paid, interest on bank loans and borrowing may be deducted if it is demonstrated that the loan was obtained and exclusively used by the Omani branch.

Foreign exchange fluctuations

Foreign exchange fluctuations arising from transactions between a branch of a foreign entity in Oman and its head office or any affiliate are generally ignored for purposes of Omani taxation. Consequently, foreign-exchange losses are not allowed, and foreign-exchange gains are not taxed.

Non-resident companies without Omani permanent establishments

If a foreign company does not have a permanent establishment in Oman, only the following categories of Omani source income are taxed:

- royalties;
- rent for equipment;
- management fees;
- fees for transfers of technical know-how;
- fees for research and development.

Income in the categories listed above is taxed at a flat rate of 10 per cent. Tax is withheld at source and remitted to the SGT.

Partnerships and joint ventures

Partnerships

Partnerships are treated as taxable entities and are taxed at corporate rates. For details concerning corporate tax rates, see Appendix A.

Joint ventures

Joint ventures are treated as taxable entities and are taxed at corporate rates. For details concerning corporate tax rates, see Appendix A. The share of after-tax profits arising from the joint venture is treated as taxed dividend income; therefore, each partner to the joint venture is not taxed again separately on such income.

Taxation of individuals

Personal income, excluding business income, is not taxable in Oman.

Only an Omani national or, under certain circumstances, a national of a GCC member country, may operate a business as a sole proprietor in Oman. Sole proprietors are taxed on Omani source income only, according to the following rates:

Net taxable income	Rate (%)
First RO30,000	0
Excess over RO30,000	12

No separate tax is levied on capital gains. Capital gains relating to acquired intangible assets or to the fixed assets of a sole proprietorship are subject to tax as business profits.

Withholding taxes

Oman does not impose withholding tax on dividends or interest.

Withholding tax at a flat rate of 10 per cent is withheld for royalties and certain other categories of income received by a foreign company that does not have an Omani permanent establishment. The payer of these types of income must withhold and remit such tax to the government on a monthly basis. Penalties are imposed for delays in payment. The withholding tax is a final tax to the recipients, and thus such recipients are not required to submit tax declarations.

Other taxes

Oman does not impose estate tax, gift tax or dividends tax. Municipalities may impose certain consumption taxes, including tax on the income categories outlined below:

- 5 per cent on hotel and restaurant bills.

- 4 per cent on hotels, motels and restaurants.

- Tax at a rate of 2 per cent on electricity bills exceeding RO50 per month.

- Tax at a rate of 3 per cent on lease agreements, payable by landlords.

Tax treaties

Oman has entered into double tax treaties with France, India, Mauritius, Pakistan, Tunisia and the United Kingdom. It has also signed tax treaties that await ratification with Algeria, Egypt and Italy.

Under Omani domestic law, withholding tax is not imposed on dividends or interest. Under the treaties, generally no withholding tax is imposed on royalties paid to companies resident in the contracting countries if such companies do not have a permanent establishment in Oman.

Appendix A: Company income tax rates

The following charts present company income tax rates for the 2001 tax year. The tax year runs from January through to December. If a company's income year falls within the tax year, the tax rates applicable to the tax year apply to the entire income year.

The following table presents the income tax rates for 100 per cent Omani-owned companies, general joint-stock companies, Omani companies (other than general joint-stock companies) with foreign participation of up to 70 per cent or more, joint investment accounts and citizens of GCC countries engaged in certain permitted economic activities.

Net taxable income	Rate (%)
First RO30,000	0
Excess over RO30,000	12

Foreign companies that do not have a permanent establishment in Oman are subject to a flat tax of 10 per cent of gross income on the following types of income: royalties; management fees; rent for equipment; fees for transfers of technical know-how; and research and development fees.

Branches of foreign companies and Omani companies with foreign participation of more than 70 per cent are taxed at a single tax rate according to the entire amount of the branch's or Omani company's taxable income, at the following tax rates.

Taxable income exceeding RO	Taxable income not exceeding RO	Rate (%)*
0	5,000	0
5,000	18,000	5
18,000	35,000	10
35,000	55,000	15
55,000	75,000	20
75,000	100,000	25
100,000	–	30

*The tax rate applies to the branch's or Omani company's entire amount of profit. For example, tax at a rate of 25 per cent applies to taxable income of RO80,000. The amount of tax due is RO20,000 (RO80,000 x 25 per cent = RO20,000). Marginal relief is available if the branch's or Omani company's taxable income slightly exceeds the tax bracket; the amount of taxable income exceeding the tax bracket is treated as tax, and is paid to the Ministry of Finance in full.

Appendix B: Depreciation rates

The following table presents acceptable depreciation rates for tax purposes.

Asset	Rate (%)
Permanent buildings	4
Prefabricated buildings	15
Bridges, platforms, pipelines, roads and railways	10
Heavy equipment	33.33
Motor vehicles	33.33
Furniture	33.33
Other equipment and tools	15
Aircraft and ships	15
Hospital buildings and educational establishments	100
Scientific research equipment	100
Intangible assets	Rate determined by the SGT

The rates must be applied to cost in accordance with straight-line depreciation. For industrial buildings, the rate is doubled. For equipment that is used continuously for three shifts a day, an accelerated rate of depreciation up to 150 per cent of the regular rate may be allowed.

Appendix C: Tax calculation for a branch of a foreign company

The following is a sample tax calculation for a branch of a foreign company.

	RO	RO
Calculation of taxable income		
Gross receipts or gross sales (RO100,500 less returns and allowances of RO500)		100,000
Less: Cost of goods sold and/or operations		(50,000)
Gross profit		50,000
Add:		
Interest and discounts	1,000	
Gross rents	1,000	
Royalties	1,000	
Balancing charges	1,000	
Income from other sources	1,000	5,000
Total income		55,000
Less allowable deductions:		
Salaries and wages	10,000	
Minor repairs and maintenance	500	
Bad debts written off*	1,000	
Rents	1,000	
Interest (on money borrowed wholly and exclusively for the purpose of producing gross income)	1,000	
Contributions to pension plans or other similar approved plans	500	
Balancing allowances	500	
Advertising	500	
Other deductions	10,000	
Total deductions		(25,000)
Taxable income before net operating loss deduction and special deductions (RO55,000 – RO25,000)		30,000
Less: Net operating loss deduction –		
Taxable income		30,000
Calculation of tax		
Tax on RO30,000 at a rate of 10%		3,000
Credit: Estimated tax paid		(2,500)
Tax due and payable		500

* Provisions are not allowed; only actual write-offs are allowed.

Part 5

The Financial Structure and Banking System

5.1

Banking Sector

Philip Dew, Philip Dew Consultancy Limited, Bahrain

Introduction

Banking in the Sultanate of Oman can be traced back to 1948, when the British Bank of the Middle East (now HSBC) opened a branch in Muscat and remained the sole banking institution in the country for the next 20 years. The Oman Currency Board was formed in 1972 and the first banking law was enacted in 1974 – when the Central Bank of Oman was also established.

Today, after a period of consolidation, there are 15 commercial banks in the Sultanate, three specialized banks and five financial and leasing companies. In addition, there are 11 money exchange companies. Of the commercial banks, six are locally incorporated, of which four are open to public subscription and two are closed companies, with the remaining nine being branches of foreign banks. All banking in Oman is overseen, regulated and closely controlled by the Central Bank (see also Chapter 5.3).

Commercial banks

The 15 banks now operating in Oman are:

- Bank Dhofar Al Omani Al Fransi.
- BankMuscat.
- National Bank of Oman Ltd.
- Oman Arab Bank.
- Oman International Bank.
- Majan International Bank.

- Bank Melli Iran.

- Bank of Baroda.

- Bank Saderat Iran.

- Banque Banorabe.

- HSBC Bank Middle East.

- Citibank NA.

- Habib Bank Ltd.

- Standard Chartered Bank.

- National Bank of Abu Dhabi.

The total assets of these banks at the end of 2001 approximated to RO4,000 million (US$10,400 million), of which amount total lending amounted to RO3,200 million (US$8,320 million). Core capital and reserves at the same date approximated to RO426 million (US$1,108 million), while deposits totalled some RO2,630 million (US$6,838 million).

The largest of the banks is BankMuscat, with total assets in excess of RO1,300 million (US$3,380 million), followed by Oman International Bank with total assets in excess of RO730 million (US$1,900 million). Between them, these two banks have approximately 50 per cent of all banking assets in Oman.

Specialized banks

The three specialized banks are the Oman Development Bank (ODB), Oman Housing Bank and Alliance Housing Bank. Until January 2002, there was also the Industrial Bank of Oman, which has now been absorbed into BankMuscat.

As will be seen in Chapter 5.6, the ODB's role is to support small and medium projects across a number of productive sectors. The two housing banks seek to provide funding to Omani nationals for the purchase of land or houses and for building or improving their homes.

Financial and leasing companies

All five financial and leasing companies are publicly quoted on the Muscat Securities Market (MSM), and they are:

- Muscat Finance Company;

- Oman Leasing Company;

- Oman Orix Leasing Company;

- Al Omaniya Financial Services;

- United Finance Company.

These companies provide an array of financial products including asset financing, leasing, and debt factoring to both private and corporate sectors. The assets financed include motor vehicles, plant and machinery, computers, and consumer durables.

Money exchange companies

The 11 money exchange companies fulfil a number of functions but their main activities are foreign exchange and remittances, particularly to the Indian Sub-Continent by lower paid workers.

Current situation

Banking in the Sultanate is in what might be described as a transition stage. Economic growth in Oman has been slow for a number of years and, allied to a heavy fall in the MSM in 1998, this has had a markedly adverse impact on the country's corporate sector. This situation, in the light of profligate lending by the banks in the early 1990s, has meant that many companies have been unable to meet their financial commitments, resulting in the banks facing numerous bad loans and the need for substantial provisioning.

The seriousness of this situation is clearly evidenced by a marked fall in bank profits in 2001. According to provisional figures issued by the Central Bank, the total profitability (after provisions) of all banks operating in Oman fell to RO38 million (US$98.8 million) in 2001 from RO64 million (US$166 million) a year earlier; an overall fall of approximately 41 per cent. These figures are a direct result of the heavy provisioning encouraged by the Central Bank in order to ensure full coverage of the banks' much publicized bad loan exposure.

Helpful though the Central Bank's intervention has been, and bankers generally applaud the move to tidy up the sector and the interrelated increase in transparency, opinions differ markedly as to how quickly the banks will be able to fully recover. With excess liquidity, limited good-quality lending opportunities and therefore higher competitive pressures, many bankers within the Gulf feel that 2002 will remain difficult for the Sultanate's banks, whereas a number of Omani bankers are more optimistic. Whatever, the introduction of International Accounting Standards (IAS), and particularly IAS 39, and membership by Oman of the World Trade Organization (WTO), which will result in the retail banking sector being opened up to international banks in 2003/2004, are thought likely to have at least some adverse impact on indigenous banks in the coming few years – although their combined effect is likely to serve to strengthen the Omani banking sector in the longer term.

5.2

Insurance Sector

*Vipin Chandra, Country Manager, Oman,
Norwich Union Insurance (Gulf) Limited,
Muscat*

The Sultanate of Oman is one of the most beautiful countries in the Arab world, with a long coastline, beautiful beaches, rugged mountains and fascinating wadis. Oman is easily reached from all parts of the world. Its people are warm and friendly, and their generous hospitality can be experienced right from the point of arriving at the international airport by plane or crossing one of their borders with the United Arab Emirates, Saudi Arabia or Yemen.

Trade has been thriving in Oman for centuries. There is evidence of commercial contact between Oman and China hundreds of years ago. Therefore, it should come as no surprise that commercial laws, including insurance law, are as developed in Oman as they are in most parts of the world.

Insurance in Oman is regulated by Royal Decree 12/1979, which came into effect in March 1979, and subsequent ministerial orders and royal decrees. The legislation is based on UK insurance law and has been amended several times since its inception. A revised regulation has been drafted to replace the existing one, which is being discussed and debated by the various ministries.

Insurance business is controlled by the Department of Insurance, which comes under the Ministry of Commerce and Industry. Premium income in 1999 was RO50.5 million (US$131.1 million), slightly lower than in 1998 when it was RO51.2 million (US$132.99 million). Non-life income is the smallest in the Gulf Cooperation Council (GCC) countries. Non-life premium to GDP is only 0.84 per cent, with per capita at RO51.80 (US$134.50).

Until early 2001, there were five national and nine foreign insurance companies. In February that year, Oman National discontinued its operations and international mergers and restructuring resulted in Axa and Northern Assurance announcing their decision to withdraw from the Oman market later the same year.

Corporate

International contractors seeking government and quasi-government business need to place their insurances with national companies. This would specifically apply to energy-related industry, development of seaports and airports. There are 12 insurance companies and 18 active brokers in the local market. This overcrowding has given rise to excess capacity, resulting in extremely thin rates. Service levels among local companies do not compare favourably with the European insurers. Many of the foreign companies employ brokers to arrange their risk management in Oman.

There are two major ports in Oman: Mina Al Sultan Qaboos in Muscat and the new port in Salalah. Both have excellent facilities. Salalah is being developed as a Free Trade Zone. Marine insurance is one of the most profitable classes of business, which speaks for the good cargo handling and excellent transportation facilities in Oman.

Warehouses are similar to those in other GCC countries and are situated close to fire hydrants and local fire brigades. However, they are still considered to be a major risk. The major exposure for insurers used to be flood risks, which in the past swept away miles of road. Underwriters remain cautious while accepting these risks even though the government has taken adequate steps to prevent such losses.

Construction of roads, power plants and other allied civil works are still the prime industrial activity in Oman outside the energy sector.

Brokers control a major share of the insurance market. Of the 18 active brokers in Oman, only two are international intermediaries operating directly and two in association with local companies. Brokers need a licence from the Ministry of Commerce and Industry to operate in Oman. They also need to provide professional indemnity cover.

Personal lines

The vehicle licensing authority in Oman is very strict. Traffic is well regulated but the incidence of traffic accidents is still high in proportion to the number of vehicles on the roads. Motor rates have risen steeply during the past two years. The government is taking steps to bring down the frequency of accidents. A recent decree from His Majesty Sultan Qaboos has stipulated stiff penalties for careless and drunken driving.

Motor insurance is compulsory in Oman and forms the bulk of non-life insurance business. In 1999, it represented 55 per cent of total premium income. Therefore, the fortunes of the motor portfolio are directly proportionate to the overall results of a company. In 1999, the motor claims ratio was just over 97 per cent. This did not include acquisition commission or management expenses!

The regulations have laid down minimum third-party coverage for motor vehicles, termed 'unified policy'. Maximum liability in the event of death is RO5,000 (US$12,887). However, permanent disability claims can reach RO35,000–RO50,000. There is no motor claims tribunal to handle these claims and all cases are dealt with by the Sharia (Islamic) Courts.

Many of the reputable companies offer wider cover than those specified by the unified policy. However, the market is not as progressive as the Dubai or Bahrain markets as no insurer offers attractive features such as a replacement car following an accident. However, there has been tremendous development in the provision of breakdown services, and if a tourist gets stuck on the mountains or in the wadis he can be certain of being rescued within a reasonable time by organizations such as AAA, who operate from major towns in Oman.

Other personal lines include travel, home and household goods (transit) insurance. The European companies dominate this segment and understandably European expatriates form the bulk of this customer segment. It is difficult to buy medical insurance for individuals in Oman. The government provides medical care free of cost to Omanis, but expatriates are now required to seek care from private hospitals or clinics.

The collapse of Oman National Insurance Company was the most significant event in the insurance market in 2001. It caused considerable concern among the insuring public and more attention is now being given to the security of the insurer than had been the case in the past. Insurance companies have also become cautious in acceptance of major risks. Customers now look for better service and better products as they are being asked to pay a higher premium, which bodes well for all parties concerned.

5.3

Banking Regulation

Roger Clarke, Regional Banking and Finance Partner, Trowers & Hamlins, Bahrain

Banking Law 2000

The original Banking Law was promulgated in 1974. It established the Central Bank of Oman with a mandate to issue currency and supervise all aspects of banking business, which included advising the Omani government on international and domestic fiscal policies. The Central Bank was entrusted with the promotion of free market expansion through the establishment of appropriate banking institutions and contribution to the fiscal and monetary development of the Sultanate through active participation in the international monetary community and membership of international monetary organizations such as the International Monetary Fund (IMF).

Royal Decree 114/2000 promulgated the new Banking Law 2000 (BL 2000). Primarily consolidating legislation, BL 2000 continued the trend of much recent legislation, which has sought to strengthen and expand Oman's free market economy and promote financial stability.

The Banking Law of 1974 was expressly repealed by Article 2 of BL 2000. That article also provides that all regulations, decisions, orders and circulars issued in implementation of the old banking law remain effective until they are repealed or amended. Most of the 1974 law has been reproduced, providing a large measure of continuity. The supervisory powers of the Central Bank were increased (e.g., key bank positions are now ratified by the Central Bank and directors have to satisfy a 'fit and proper' test). The Central Bank's scope now covers more activities than previously (codes of conduct with regard to investment powers, confidentiality of transactions and duties of officers and employees were included). The new law also raised the minimum capital of Omani banks from RO10 million (US$26 million) to RO20 million (US$52 million), and that of a branch of a foreign bank to RO3 million (US$7.8 million). In addition, the Central Bank's role in advising the government on matters of domestic and international affairs was also enhanced.

The Central Bank is independent from the apparatus of the State. As a result, it operates with greater freedom than government ministries. The powers that it derives from BL 2000 give the Central Bank almost unfettered control over the banking sector within Oman.

The management of the Central Bank is entrusted to a board of governors. The board has full authority to perform all acts required for the management and operation of the Central Bank and the supervision of banking business in the Sultanate. The board consists of seven governors, each of whom is appointed by the Sultan. The management powers of the board of governors are very broad and include:

- examining account books, records and other affairs of any licensed bank;

- delegating investigation of banking activity and operation to a third party;

- reviewing reports prepared by licensed banks which are required by the Central Bank from time to time to monitor banking practice;

- allowing licensed banks to establish branches;

- taking all such actions as are required to supervise properly and regulate banking in the Sultanate;

- regulating and supervising all matters relating to the currency of the Sultanate, including printing and issuing notes, licensing and suspending the licences of any licensed banks, or imposing sanctions on banks which fail to comply with the directives and policies issued by the Central Bank;

- promulgating regulations of the Central Bank related to all aspects of banking business in the Sultanate.

The Central Bank has the power to appoint an administrator to take over a bank's operations in certain circumstances, including a Central Bank-perceived risk of bank failure, non-payment and violation of the Banking Law or regulations. The Central Bank also has the power to suspend banking licences.

Banking regulation

Any bank wishing to set up in Oman must obtain a licence from the Central Bank (Article 52 of BL 2000). The licence will specify the banking activities that individual banks may undertake.

The prescribed corporate form for a bank is that of a joint-stock company (Article 55(b) of BL 2000). This may be a closed joint-stock company (SAOC), which does not offer its shares for public subscription, or an open joint-stock company (SAOG), which does. Most banks in

Oman were established as SAOCs, but many of them have converted to the latter to take advantage of the additional funds which public subscription generates.

Foreign banks may, with Central Bank approval, establish in Oman (Article 52 of BL 2000). The Central Bank maintains the same regulatory functions over foreign banks as it does over domestic banks. This includes, but is not limited to, imposing lending ratios and capital adequacy requirements on these banks.

A foreign bank wishing to set up in Oman must submit a copy of its constitutional documents and proof that it has the authority to engage in banking business within its own jurisdiction (Article 53(3) of BL 2000). It should provide details of the proposed banking business that it will undertake in Oman and any other information required in connection with its application as requested by the Central Bank, which reviews this application. The bank must submit all other documents required by other legislation in force in Oman and by other government departments (Article 53(6) of BL 2000).

Capital deposit

All licensed banks must make a capital deposit with the Central Bank before commencing business (Article 61 of BL 2000). This deposit should be maintained at a level of at least 10 per cent of the deposits made (Article 61(b)).

Deposit insurance scheme

A deposit insurance scheme was set up by Royal Decree 9/1995 (as amended by Royal Decree 111/2000). The regulations implementing the scheme were issued as BM 759. This scheme is designed to provide insurance coverage for 75 per cent of a deposit or RO20,000 (US$52,000) (whichever is less) on all deposits with banks operating in the Sultanate and to boost confidence in the banking system and minimize the risk factors associated with it.

Lending ratios and limits

From time to time, the Central Bank issues regulations relating to lending ratios. The current level of this ratio stands at 87.5 per cent of its deposits (BM 887). No licensed bank shall lend, whether by way of loan, discount, advance and/or overdraft, whether secured or unsecured, when such lending in aggregate exceeds 87.5 per cent of its total deposits.

The level of consumer loans is limited to 40 per cent of the bank's private sector credit (BM 924, 31 December 2001). Such loans are classified as those granted to an individual for non-productive, non-business purposes, which may include, but are not limited to, the purchase of automobiles and other goods not exceeding RO9,000 (US$23,400).

The Banking Law 1974 provided that 10 per cent of the net worth of the bank was the maximum level of exposure to an individual borrower. This level was raised to 15 per cent by Royal Decree 69/1991. The maximum level of 10 per cent is maintained for senior members of the management of the bank (confirmed in BM 889). The aggregate lending to all senior members in management of the bank collectively must not exceed 35 per cent.

With regard to foreign branches of Omani banks, their lending limit to foreign corporations or persons should not exceed 5 per cent of its global net worth. This is in line with the requirement that the total exposure of the bank to foreign entities or persons should not exceed 5 per cent of its global net worth.

Other provisions

Capital adequacy

The Central Bank has set a capital adequacy ratio of 12 per cent (Bank for International Settlements is 8 per cent).

Foreign investment

No bank shall invest more than 2.5 per cent of its net worth in foreign bonds, notes and debentures (Article 65(b)(1) of BL 2000). In addition, no licensed bank may invest more than 5 per cent of its net worth in securities of corporations that are domiciled outside the Sultanate (Article 65(b)(4) of BL 2000). There is a ceiling of US$1 million on banks' equity-related investments in international stock markets (BM 886). Banks should operate a stop loss of 10 per cent with regard to any foreign trading portfolio of shares (BM 876).

Interest rates

The Central Bank imposes ceilings on the interest rates that can be charged by licensed banks on personal loans. BM 924 set the level at 12 per cent per year, effective 1 January 2002.

Restrictions on directors, officers and managers

Article 80(b) of BL 2000 states that without the express authorization of the Central Bank, no person who is a director of a licensed bank may hold any office in another bank nor accept office on the board of directors of any commercial company if such office is in conflict with his responsibilities under this law.

Restrictions on shareholding in local banks

BM 807 (incorporating Reg/40/96) restricts the shareholding of any individuals and their related parties within local banks. Article 1 stipulates that the aggregate holding must not exceed 15 per cent of the voting shares in a locally incorporated bank. Similarly, the aggregate holding by an incorporated body and its related parties must not exceed 25 per cent of the voting shares, and that held by a joint-stock or holding company must not exceed 35 per cent.

Restrictions on banks holding shares and debentures

Under Article 65(b)(1) of BL 2000, subject to certain limitations, a bank may purchase, hold and sell for its own account debt instruments provided that the aggregate value of such investments does not exceed 10 per cent of the net worth of the bank and investment in any particular security does not exceed 5 per cent.

Similarly, under Article 65(b)(3)(4) of BL 2000, a bank may hold shares in government-formed companies provided these shares do not exceed 5 per cent of the bank's net worth. The bank may also invest up to 20 per cent of its net worth in other shares subject to certain exceptions and provided that no single holding exceeds 5 per cent of the shares in a corporation.

Conclusion

The Central Bank is keen to maintain the international standard of banking for banks in Oman. The Central Bank approves the international convergence of bank supervisory standards and attempts to adopt them for the Omani banking system. The regulation of banking institutions which are either incorporated in Oman or which are permitted to carry on business through branches or subsidiaries is carried out in accordance with internationally accepted standards for the regulation of financial institutions, and there is increasing cooperation and regulation of cross-border financial institutions to ensure that they maintain acceptable standards and comply with home supervisory regulatory requirements.

5.4

Muscat Securities Market (MSM)

Ahmed AlMarhoon, General Manager,
Muscat Securities Market, Ruwi

The Muscat Securities Market (MSM) was established in 1989 by Royal Decree 53/1988, which set the legal framework for the establishment of the market as an independent organization to regulate and control the Omani securities market and to participate with other organizations in setting up the infrastructure of the Sultanate's financial sector. In early 1998, a new Capital Market Law came into effect, which split the former MSM into three independent entities: the exchange itself (MSM); a regulatory authority, Capital Market Authority (CMA); and a central depository, Muscat Depository & Securities Registration Company (MDSRC).

MSM members now include public corporations, listed companies, intermediaries and the Central Bank of Oman.

Regulatory reforms and technical improvements have enhanced the status of MSM as the region's leading stock exchange, enabling it to play a major role in attracting private investment.

Capital Market Authority (CMA)

The Capital Market Authority (CMA) is a government body charged with regulating the exchange, the central depository and the capital markets and their participants. The CMA administers and enforces Capital Market Law, Royal Decree 80/1998, which empowers it to:

- organize, license and monitor the issue and trading of securities;

- supervise the operations of the MSM;

- supervise all companies operating in the field of securities.
  (See also Chapter 5.5.)

Muscat Depository & Securities Registration Company (MDSRC)

The Muscat Depository & Securities Registration Company (MDSRC) commenced operation in February 1999 following the issue of Royal Decree 82/1998. It is a closed joint-stock company and is the sole provider in the Sultanate for registration services, transfer of ownership of securities and safekeeping of ownership documents.

The MDSRC maintains and continually updates the records of share ownership as shares are bought and sold. Most share records are kept in book form and are updated automatically through the electronic trading system. As the central transfer agent, registrar and depository, the MDSRC's role is to ensure the efficient settlement of trades, the maintenance of accurate records and the facilitation of corporate actions.

Electronic trading

A computerized system run by Andersen Consulting (now Accenture) of the United States commenced operations at the beginning of 1997 and electronic trading commenced in July 1998. Settlement takes place on the basis of T+3. The system creates an environment for different market entities to trade in listed companies via high-technology computers regardless of their actual locations. It also contributes to the continuous development of the stock exchange by providing a fair and transparent market and enabling full dissemination of information to all trading entities immediately.

For the purpose of trading on MSM, there are three market categories in which joint-stock companies are listed:

- Regular Market;
- Parallel Market;
- Third Market.

Regular Market

Public joint-stock companies can be listed on the Regular Market if they satisfy the following requirements:

- Paid-up capital must not be less than RO2 million.
- Shareholders' equity must not be less than 100 per cent of the paid-up capital.

- Irrespective of the legal form under which they operate, such companies must have been in operation for a minimum of three years, and have published audited financial statements for each year of operation prepared in accordance with International Accounting Standards (IAS).

- They must have achieved net profits within each of the last three years preceding the application for listing or transfer to the Regular Market.

Parallel Market

Public joint-stock companies can be listed on the Parallel Market if they satisfy the following requirements:

- Regardless of the legal form under which they operate and prior to the application for listing or transferring to the Parallel Market, such companies must have been in operation for a minimum of three years, and have published audited financial statements prepared in accordance with IAS.

- They must have achieved a net profit during the year preceding the date of the listing application and their paid-up capital must have been decreased to more than 50 per cent, or they must have achieved profit within one of the last three years and maintained their paid-up capital at the end of the year preceding submission of the listing application.

- They have been transferred from the Regular or Third Market.

- They are other securities deemed suitable by the CMA to be listed on this Market.

Third Market

The following companies can be listed on the Third Market:

- Public joint-stock companies that do not satisfy the requirements for listing on the Regular and Parallel Markets.

- Closed joint-stock companies.

- Companies whose listing has been transferred from the Regular or Parallel Markets.

- Any other securities deemed suitable by the CMA to be listed on the Third Market.

Bond Market

The government started issuing development bonds in 1991. Regulations permitting the issue of corporate bonds have yet to be published.

Foreign investment

Foreign institutions and individuals are permitted to invest in Omani companies. It is now the CMA's requirement that all companies seeking a listing must agree to be open to all foreign investors who can invest in equities on the MSM via brokers. There are no taxes on dividends or capital gains, and no limits on repatriation of profits.

Taxation

In 1996, amendments were made to the Companies Tax Law aimed at encouraging Omani joint-stock companies to allow non-Omani shareholders. Previously, companies with non-Omani shareholders paid a higher rate of tax than those which were 100 per cent Omani-owned. This was changed so that companies with up to 49 per cent non-Omani ownership – the highest level permitted under the Foreign Capital Investment Law (FCIL) – are now treated as wholly Omani-owned companies.

Key developments

Since the beginning of 2000, the Omani authorities have been active in instituting a wide-ranging package of measures aimed at revitalizing and strengthening the stock market.

Performance

Between 1989 and 1994, the MSM share market index, which comprised 50 stocks, rose 46 per cent. In 1995, it rose 8 per cent and in 1996 it appreciated by 26 per cent. In 1997, it appreciated by 141 per cent to make MSM the world's second best-performing market after the Budapest Stock Exchange. On 3 February 1998, the market hit a record of 509.84, after which it slipped back. The MSM index ended 1998 at 228.47, which was 55 per cent down on its February peak.

The downward trend continued in 1999 and the general index hit a cyclical low of 209.16 at the end of March that year. Following the oil price recovery, there was a rebound in prices and the index reached

292.27 at the end of July 1999. However, the market was hit by regular selling as investors sought to recoup losses by selling as prices firmed. As a result, the general index went into reverse again in the second half of that year. The index ended at 250.20, up 9.54 per cent on its year-end 1999 value. 2000 marked another troubled year for the MSM as investors failed to respond in any significant fashion to repeated government measures aimed at the market's rejuvenation.

The total market capitalization for all securities listed in the market on 31 December 2000 was RO1.948 billion, which was approximately equivalent to US$5 billion.

Despite the extreme fluctuations in the market over the last three years, it is notable that levels of foreign investment have remained virtually stable at around 14–15 per cent of total share ownership of quoted companies in 1998–2000.

Recognized excellence

Regulatory reforms and technical improvements have enhanced the status of the MSM as the region's leading stock exchange, enabling it to play a major role in attracting private investment.

The key change has been structural. Instead of a single organization, there are now three, with the CMA acting as an independent regulator, the MSM running the exchange and the MDSRC in charge of depository and transfer functions. 'The time has clearly come to separate trade, regulatory and depository functions in line with best international practices. We think this is the proper way to run a capital market because it brings transparency and efficiency,' says Yahya al-Jabri, executive president of the CMA.

The exchange has also pressed ahead with technical changes, including an electronic trading system that allows automated order matching, online market control, and remote order, as well as making possible online cross-listing with other exchanges.

The 12-year-old MSM is the first exchange in any of the Gulf States to introduce technical and regulatory changes of this sort. The measures, as well as an earlier decision to become the first exchange in the Gulf to allow the participation of foreign investors, have helped Muscat establish a reputation as one of the region's most progressive, best regulated, and most transparent capital markets. Sixteen brokerage houses operate on the MSM, which has approximately 200,000 investors.

Further improvements, led by the introduction of global depositary receipts and an agreement to list some Omani shares on the London Stock Exchange, are planned. A central stock payment system will speed settlements and help brokers' cash flow, while the MSM and depository companies are developing a programme to streamline the distribution of dividend payments. The CMA also wants to upgrade brokers' qualifications.

Attracting investors is of crucial importance to Oman, whose development strategy is based on a dynamic private sector. Some shares in public-sector industries such as telecommunications and electricity generation enterprises will also be floated on the exchange.

Equally important, the reforms will further strengthen a market that is again on the upswing. Share prices climbed throughout most of the 1990s, peaking in 1997 with a 141 per cent gain in the index, but followed by a 40 per cent correction in 1998, blamed on the drop in oil prices. The total market capitalization at the end of October 1999 was RO1.723 billion (US$4.46 billion), with 140 companies listed.

Capital Market Authority (CMA)

Capital Market Authority, Ruwi

Introduction

Before 1998, the Muscat Securities Market (MSM) was from the outset one entity comprising the regulator (the supervisory body) and the stock exchange, where trading securities (selling and buying) took place. Experience showed that such an integration weakened the supervisory role of the market as the staff were preoccupied with the matters of trading, settlement, depository services, transfer and the related daily problems at the expense of both the supervisory role and market development. Therefore, the Omani government took the decision to separate the supervisory body from the stock exchange and depository. Thus, in 1998, Royal Decree 80/1998 promulgating the Capital Market Law separated the supervisory body from the stock exchange and Royal Decree 82/1998 established Muscat Depository & Securities Registration Company (MDSRC) in the form of a closed joint-stock company.

The Capital Market Authority's mission is to upgrade the efficiency of the Capital Market in the Sultanate and protect investors from unjust and unsound practices. The CMA is empowered to:

- organize licences and monitor the issue and trading of securities;

- supervise the operations of the MSM;

- supervise all companies operating in the field of securities.

In order to accomplish its mission, the CMA was established as an independent government agency and given statutory powers to implement its role under law.

Recently, the environment surrounding both securities regulation and the securities market in Oman has changed considerably. The CMA supervises and regulates one of the most accessible of Arab stock markets – indeed, one of the region's most progressive markets – while also being the best regulated and most transparent capital market in the region.

Regulatory landscape

The Capital Market Law, which came into effect in 1998, made some far-reaching changes to the regulatory framework governing the securities market in Oman. This has resulted in greater legal and regulatory certainty in the area of public offerings of securities – a move towards promoting a more efficient and competitive capital market. The Capital Market Law and its amendment state that it is now incumbent on issuers to provide sufficient and accurate disclosure of all material information to investors and their advisers to enable them to evaluate the risks and merits of their investment. Under this law, the licensing regime is more rigorous in licensing all intermediaries and brokerage firms, companies acting as intermediaries, and those providing other financial market services. As the regulator, the CMA has the power to intervene directly in the management of a company by appointing an observer to the board or by dissolving the board and appointing a custodian to manage the company pending the election of a new board. In the interests of shareholder protection, the Capital Market Law expressly forbids insider trading and price manipulation, while giving the company, shareholders and third parties the right to recover damages against directors if the latter are responsible for fraud, negligence or other legal violations.

Some of the high points of the law in the interests of shareholders are:

- the right to impose criminal penalties in certain cases;

- mandatory arbitration of disputes between 'persons dealing in the securities field';

- the setting-up of a Grievances Committee made up of three members: two professional judges nominated by the president of the Commercial Court and the third from the CMA, who must be an officer with the rank of at least director-general. The jurisdiction of the committee is primarily administrative, in that it is given competence to determine objections to decisions on securities market matters that are rendered by the regulatory bodies – but its determinations are final.

In addition, due to the CMA's desire to enhance disclosure, which is an important element in order to establish transparency; to create confidence in securities investment; and to maintain fair and sound bases of dealing wherein all types of investors have equal opportunities, the CMA issued new rules for disclosure. Under the Disclosure Rules, all audited and unaudited accounts must include and fairly present all material information relevant to understanding the company's financial position and performance during a given period. All changes in accounting policies between periods must also be clearly disclosed. Moreover, every publicly quoted shareholding company must establish, maintain and enforce written policies, procedures and systems of supervision reasonably designed to ensure the fair and timely release of material information about the company and, also, ensure that the information it releases about the company is correct, timely and reasonably complete.

Improving the competitiveness of the market

While working to further develop and strengthen the overall Capital Market, the need to rectify structural weaknesses and enhance the competitiveness of the stock-broking industry was not overlooked. Indeed, the CMA's experience throughout the earlier years clearly highlighted the deterioration in the sector; many of the brokerages were small and survived mainly as niche players. The need to redress the situation prompted the CMA to initiate a merger programme so as to reduce the number of small firms and produce stronger, well-capitalized players robust enough to withstand the risks inherent in the business and sufficiently well-prepared to face the challenges of globalization and liberalization. Progress in regard to consolidation has been fairly encouraging, as the brokers have come to realize the merits of merger and consolidation.

In addition, a decision was taken to reduce the settlement period, which reduces the level of risk and increases market efficiency. The implementation of the T+3 settlement period on the MSM will put this exchange on a par with international exchanges, thus making it more comparable and competitive.

Enhancing transparency and governance in the Capital Market

Within the Capital Market, future market regulation, which facilitates innovation and growth, also addresses investor protection and prudential concerns effectively. The adoption of a market-based approach to regulation represents a clear paradigm shift on the part of the CMA towards greater use of competitive market disciplines and processes, with minimum direct regulatory intervention in pursuit of its objectives. To a degree, elements of the CMA's regulations have been reflected in the gradual shift, which began in 1998, from the merit-review process for the public offering of securities to disclosure regulation, which relies on higher standards of disclosure and accountability by issuers. Such a regulatory environment will provide for more efficient pricing, greater transparency and liquidity and will help in meeting investor expectations through full disclosure of information by companies whose securities are being traded. To these ends, the CMA is continuously updating its rules and regulations based on studies and surveys of the market and on public comment and feedback.

Enforcing the law

Working with an enforcement regime that recognizes no constraints of fear or favour, the CMA continues to act against breaches of the Capital Market Law and regulations. The CMA deals with all complaints that are received and adheres closely to Chapter Four of the Capital Market Law, which clearly defines the responsibilities of the Appeals and Disciplinary Committee. The policy-makers within the CMA believe that the law itself means nothing if it is not implemented in a wise, honest and equitable manner among all market participants

Technology: implications for the capital market

Oman is living through a digital revolution. With the advent of computing and communication technologies, a networked and borderless world is forming, geographical barriers are disappearing and speed is of the essence. This is the world of what has been called the 'New Economy': technology driven, knowledge based and fast moving. The new economy resulting from the rise of IT has generated several dynamics that impact on the nature of capital market structures and operations. Therefore, the CMA pays much attention to implementing the new technology and to updating its systems and methods. In this regard, the CMA has set up its own website and has implemented an electronic securities trading system on the MSM, as well as electronic registration and storing of information so as to provide timely information to all investors around the world.

CMA: an expanding international role

Within the CMA it is believed that, with increasing globalization and inter-penetrability of capital markets, international regulatory cooperation has become a matter of great priority, particularly if Oman is to achieve its ambition of becoming a world-class financial market. The CMA has always been involved in international regulatory and development cooperation and is a member of many world financial organizations such as the International Organization of Securities Commissions (IOSCO) and the Arab Exchange Association, in addition to taking an active involvement in the many international forums, conferences, seminars and workshops that now fill up the calendar.

Internal developments

Several changes were made to the organizational structure of the CMA to enable it to perform its work in an effective and efficient way. In addition to its own experts, the CMA is cooperating with world advisory organizations in setting up its organizational structure. The CMA has also initiated a Research and Development Department, which plays an important role in improving the competitiveness of the securities market in the Sultanate. Finally, the CMA will continue its strategy of liaison with securities markets abroad for the purpose of exchanging information and expertise to keep up with progress.

The CMA is continuously upgrading the efficiency of its staff by organizing internal and external training programmes. These programmes provide the CMA with qualified and efficient staff who are able to participate in improving and developing its services.

Setting a clear direction for capital market development

The task before the CMA, therefore, is to soldier on over many fronts to strengthen the Oman Capital Market and develop its resilience to withstand shocks arising from volatile oil prices and economic performance. The CMA anticipates that it will indeed face interesting times ahead amid the increasingly dynamic and competitive global environment, and it has, therefore, been preparing its master plan, which was due to be finished in March 2002, in order to clarify all the organization's future steps and development strategies, thereby ensuring continuous development and the trust of investors worldwide.

Oman Development Bank (ODB)

Abdul Aziz Mohamed Al Hinai, Acting General Manager, Oman Development Bank, Muscat

Introduction and legal status

The Oman Development Bank (ODB) was established on 9 April 1997 under Royal Decree 18/1997 as an Omani joint-stock company wholly owned by the government of the Sultanate of Oman. This entity was formed as a result of the merger of two banks: Oman Development Bank, established by royal decree in 1978 and majority-owned by the government, and the 100 per cent government-owned Oman Bank of Agriculture and Fisheries, formed in 1981.

The present Oman Development Bank and the earlier merged entities were partners in the development of the manufacturing sector in Oman, which helped Oman's non-oil exports to increase from RO10.6 million (US$27.6 million) in 1983 to RO247.8 million (US$644.3 million) in 2000. In addition, the ODB was deeply involved in the expansion of infrastructure for the development and growth of other sectors of the national economy.

Principal activities

The ODB provides loans to development projects which are directly related to the various economic sectors and service industries in the field of agriculture, livestock, fisheries, tourism, education (colleges, institutes and schools), health (medical treatment and diagnostic services), professional offices, export, craft and workshops, among others.

In addition, the ODB also manages:

- the disbursement and collection of government loans approved prior to the merger in 1997;

- the disbursement of amounts from the Fisheries Research Fund.

Liquidity

The ODB was established with a share capital of RO20 million (US$52 million), which is held by the government. Other principal funding sources include borrowings from banks and financial institutions. Under the royal decree establishing the ODB, the government guarantees the bank's borrowings up to four times its capital and general reserves.

Credit activity

The ODB grants loans not exceeding RO165,000 (US$429,000) to projects whose total investment cost does not exceed RO250,000 (US$650,000). Hence, the ODB is a specialized institution lending to small and medium-sized projects situated within Oman.

The maximum loan that the ODB can lend to any one project may not exceed 150 per cent of the paid-up capital of the project if it is located inside the governorate of Muscat (except the province (wilayat) of Quriyat) and 250 per cent if the project is situated outside the governorate of Muscat or inside the province of Quriyat. However, the maximum amount that the ODB can disburse should not exceed the specified amount in the above paragraph.

The period of repayment should not exceed five years, with the possibility of granting a grace period that may extend up to two years, which makes a total term of seven years. Repayment of the loan can be made monthly, quarterly, half-yearly or on an annual basis, depending on the nature and size of the project.

Borrowers can avail of a loan for any of the following purposes:

- to establish a new project;

- to support an existing project which faces difficulties in continuing in production or rendering its service for wholly valid reasons;

- to support additional capital expenditure costs related to expansion of the production capacity of a project or to improve the services that it renders.

To encourage craftsmen and small investors, the ODB also advances small loans not exceeding RO5,000 (US$13,000) free of interest in accordance with the term and conditions laid down.

Table 5.6.1 ODB loans and advances, 2001

Sector	RO million
Services	14.983
Agriculture and fisheries	14.872
Chemical industries	5.318
Food processing and beverages	4.712
Metal products	4.148
Construction	2.487
Paper and packaging	1.710
Textiles and clothing	1.405
Furniture	0.334
Miscellaneous	0.280
Total	*50.249 (=US$130.65 million)*

Source: Oman Development Bank

Table 5.6.1 gives a brief summary by economic sector of the loans and advances disbursed by the ODB by the end of 2001.

Fisheries Research Fund

The ODB acts as a trustee for the Fisheries Research Fund, formed by Royal Decree 51/1991 and utilized for the development of fisheries research.

Oman is blessed with a vast coastline and the fisheries sector is one that can be expected to generate additional revenue for the economy. Any research projects that can help in the development of this sector can obtain financial assistance from this fund.

5.7

Role of the Export Credit Guarantee Agency (ECGA) in Promoting Omani Non-Oil Exports and its Future Outlook

Nasir bin Issa Al Ismaily, General Manager, Export Credit Guarantee Agency, Muscat

The Export Credit Guarantee Agency (ECGA) commenced export credit insurance operations in November 1991. Prior to that time, it had been known as the Export Guarantee & Financing Unit (EGFU) operating under the umbrella of the Oman Development Bank (ODB), but was renamed the Export Credit Guarantee Agency in August 1999. It is unique as the only national export credit agency within the Gulf Cooperation Council (GCC) region. It has a capital of RO7 million (US$18.2 million) and is now independent of the Oman Development Bank.

The ECGA provides credit insurance cover against commercial or buyer risks as well as non-commercial or political risks. The commercial risks that are covered by the ECGA's export credit insurance policy include insolvency/bankruptcy, default to pay, as well as non-acceptance of goods by the buyer. With regard to country risks, these include foreign exchange transfer delays, import bans or cancellation of import licence, payment moratorium, war, civil disorder and natural disasters.

When the ECGA commenced normal operations in 1992, it faced the sizeable challenge of how to sell an intangible, unique credit insurance service in a country where it had not been known before. Omani businessmen have traditionally traded with buyers on trust and thus they failed to see the need for obtaining credit insurance protection against their receivables. As a result, the ECGA had to convince exporters and others of the quantifiable and tangible benefits to be derived from credit insurance services. To this end, the ECGA also involved the banking sector in promoting the product to exporters. The cooperation and support provided by the commercial banks in jointly promoting the export credit insurance scheme to prospective clients was of utmost importance in the early days and ensured its success in the country.

The ECGA's role is more that of a catalyst through insuring exports while assisting exporters in obtaining the necessary financing from commercial banks at more favourable interest rates. The availability of cheaper financing has had a profound, positive effect as the number of exporters interested in insuring their exports with the ECGA has increased and, through the reduction in the cost of post-shipment financing through bill discounting with commercial banks, they have recognized the benefits that can be derived. Hence, in the earlier period of operations, most policyholders were more interested in cheaper funding than credit insurance.

However, as the result of the Gulf crisis, and considering the number of exporters adversely affected at that time, they realized that credit insurance was an important option. Indeed, the crisis was a blessing in disguise as credit insurance now became considered an essential tool in mitigating the risks of non-payment from buyers and, subsequently, the number of policyholders requesting credit insurance grew substantially. Thus, the primary objective of the ECGA in promoting Omani exports through the provision of credit insurance services was attained. Hence, credit insurance has long been recognized by the management of most companies as an essential and integral element in safeguarding against both commercial and non-commercial (political) risks. It has allowed exporters to venture and trade with new buyers and also enter non-traditional markets.

In addition to export credit insurance and post-shipment financing with commercial banks against discounted bills, in 1999 the ECGA introduced the Pre-shipment Export Credit Guarantee for the benefit of small-sized exporters, which allowed the commercial banks to extend working capital financing for the purchase of the raw materials needed to manufacture their products against confirmed purchase orders from abroad. Thus, the guarantee fills the security gap needed by the exporters' banks.

The operations of the ECGA since commencement of its activities have clearly been appropriate, being highly valued by exporters, with the Agency experiencing encouraging and excellent responses in the provision of its export credit insurance services. The ECGA has been successful in meeting its targets for export credit insurance business in its drive to promote Omani exports, which statement can broadly be supported by substantial increases in Omani non-oil exports from RO79.1 million (US$205.7 million) in 1991 to RO247.8 million (US$644.3

million) in 2000. The ECGA has been able to contribute to such remarkable growth as it has allowed Omani exporters to expand their export sales to new buyers and far away foreign markets in addition to GCC countries, knowing that the risks of non-payment of export shipments are insured and therefore minimized.

The ECGA has long continued to provide export credit insurance support to a large number of Omani exporters. With its credit insurance scheme, the Omani exporters are provided not only with protection against payment risks but also advice on the creditworthiness of overseas buyers and on how to collect and recover overdue bad debts. It allows exporters to sell safely on credit terms and compete effectively against other suppliers and also gives them the confidence to sell to new and far away or non-traditional markets. By insuring their exports with the ECGA, policyholders have better control over their export receivables by maintaining control of their buyers under the credit limits approved by the Agency.

Apart from risk minimization, which the exporter benefits through payment of claims by ECGA in case of non-payment by the buyers, the Export Credit Policy can also be assigned to the exporters' banks as collateral. Such assignment provides opportunities for policyholders to obtain new or enhanced post-shipment financing facilities on better or concessional terms than the banks might otherwise have been prepared to offer if the exporter was not credit insured or the policy was not available. Thus, the Export Credit Policy not only minimizes the risk of non-payment to the exporter but also assists him in obtaining necessary and better export financing terms. Hence, it provides exporters with greater financial liquidity in managing their foreign receivable portfolios.

The ECGA introduced its quarterly *News Bulletin* in 1997, which is highly informative as it provides information to exporters on the benefits of credit insurance; lists questions and answers; details cases and scenarios on claims; and provides news items pertaining to the ECGA and exports as well as useful articles on effective credit management tools for export businesses.

The ECGA has continued to attract interest among lead re-insurers through its international reinsurance treaties against both commercial and political risks, which have been highly commended. The ECGA first obtained its Quota Share Reinsurance Treaty with the group of lead re-insurers in 1996, and was the first Arab export credit agency to obtain such reinsurance protection against both commercial and political risks. The continued growth and exposure of the ECGA has been ensured since that time. The ECGA has also obtained additional reinsurance support through its association with Coface in the Credit Alliance Network. Such reinsurance support is essential considering the rapid growth of the ECGA's exposure, which stood at RO117.1 million (US$304.5 million) at the end of 2000.

The ECGA is able to actively access credit information reports from the Coface database, which enables access to the details of millions of buyers to which the ECGA is linked by an online computer system, as well as enabling underwriting decisions for higher amounts to be reinsured through Coface. In addition, the ECGA benefits from technical collaboration and assistance with debt collection and recoveries.

The ECGA was honoured by the Credit Alliance in being awarded the John Manners Memorial Shield Award during its annual meeting in September 2001 in Vienna, Austria. The ECGA was the first recipient of the award in the history of the Credit Alliance. ECGA's representation as a reappointed member to the General Steering Committee of the Credit Alliance Network under the auspices of Coface in 2000 served as an important international recognition of its status, particularly as the first Arab export credit agency to be represented on such an important committee.

ECGA was also re-elected as a Regional Coordinator for the Middle East and Africa during the annual meeting in Vienna. The Regional Committee consists of various export credit agencies in the Middle East and Africa that are already members of the Credit Alliance.

The ECGA is also a full member of the Prague Club, which is a meeting of participating export credit agencies under the auspices of the Secretariat of the Berne Union – the International Union of Credit & Investment Insurers. The ECGA's status since 2000 has been elevated from that of observer to fully fledged member.

The ECGA's experience over its 10-year history in providing vital services for the benefit of Omani exporters – whether in terms of risk minimization through credit insurance, in improving their liquidity through bill discounting under the post-shipment financing scheme, or through availability of needed working capital financing through the ECGA's Pre-shipment Export Credit Guarantee Scheme – has contributed immensely to the promotion and encouragement of Omani non-oil exports.

With regard to prospects and the proposed outlook for the future, the ECGA envisages continuation of sustained growth of its credit insurance business by meeting the increasing needs of Omani exporters for credit insurance protection against both commercial and non-commercial risks. It also envisages new challenges and opportunities in the credit insurance industry due to globalization, liberalization of trade, increased competition and the crumbling of national barriers due to the opening of markets worldwide. Such trends are expected to increase as more countries join the World Trade Organization (WTO), of which Oman became a member in 2000.

The ECGA anticipates greater integration within the Credit Alliance by actively availing various services through its platform as well as being actively engaged in marketing different products in coordination with

Coface and other partners within the Alliance. These include a range of credit insurance services and products such as the international global policy and the @ rating products.

The ECGA expects in the future to introduce domestic credit insurance as a logical extension of its credit insurance business so as to enable fulfilment of the needs and requirements of exporters rather than restricting such services solely to export. This will not only benefit the policyholders in terms of managing all their credit receivables through risk minimization and improving their liquidity and turnover, but will also enhance the ECGA's total insurable business income, thus enabling the continued attraction of international re-insurers and enabling provision of reinsurance protection to the ECGA's growing exposure against both commercial and non-commercial risks resulting from a higher volume of premiums.

In addition, the ECGA expects to promote the use of the Internet by policyholders, other potential clients and exporters, through communicating and transacting business with ECGA through web-based applications. The Internet and e-mail are expected to be key to future relationships with clients and also with their other business suppliers and associates. Thus, policyholders will be expected in the future to declare their monthly export business or requests for credit limits to the ECGA, which will then be in a position to invoice them for the premium online, thereby substituting unnecessary paperwork and improving efficiency. Concerted effort will definitely be required from both sides in order to appreciate the benefits of business-to-business (B2B) transactions, particularly when considering that the usage of e-commerce is still in its infancy in the Gulf region when compared with other developed markets. For this, there remains a need for proper preparation to meet such challenges.

Furthermore, credit insurance is expected to be continuously viewed exclusively by the policyholders as an essential tool, which provides added value through protection against the risks of non-payment, despite the need for policyholders to pay a premium for such services. That said, it is envisaged that credit insurance will stand on its own merits and be seen to provide benefits such as the policy being viewed by commercial banks as additional security assigned to them for extending pre-shipment as well as post-shipment financing facilities at better concessional lending rates due to the substantial reduction in the risk involved.

Finally, the ECGA belongs to a number of regional and international credit insurance organizations. These include forums of export credit agencies of Arab countries under the auspices of the Inter-Arab Investment Guarantee Corporation (IAIGC); of the Islamic countries under the Islamic Corporation for the Insurance of Investment and Export Credit (ICIEC); and of the Credit Alliance Network under the auspices of Coface of France. It is also a member of the Prague Club. It is to be expected that, once the ECGA meets the minimum requirements in terms of business declared and volume of premium, it will also qualify to be a fully fledged member of the Berne Union.

5.8

Omani Centre for Investment Promotion and Export Development (OCIPED): Partner in Progress

Omani Centre for Investment Promotion and Export Development

Introduction

Among the fastest growing economies of the world, the Sultanate of Oman is a vibrant blend of tradition and modernity. With a centuries-old global trading heritage, Oman is well placed to take advantage of opportunities in the new global economy, and the Omani Centre for Investment Promotion and Export Development (OCIPED) has been established to assist private-sector development in the Sultanate.

Its mission is to boost both local and international private-sector investment in key economic sectors in Oman and to work in partnership with businesses located in Oman to develop the export of goods and services to key geographical markets.

OCIPED is the first government body in the Sultanate, and only the second public-sector organization in the entire Arab world, to receive the coveted International Organization for Standardization ISO 9002 certification. This ensures that it is committed to providing its clients with the quality of service that meets their requirements, in an efficient and effective manner and within stipulated time frames.

Structure and functions

In keeping with its mission, OCIPED has two main operating divisions: the Directorate General of Investment and the Directorate General of Export Development.

The Directorate General of Investment acts as a fast track to establishing projects in Oman. It identifies and assesses project opportunities and can secure for project promoters all the necessary licences and permissions needed to operate in Oman. It also provides assistance in accessing project funding through its wide network of contacts with both local and international financial institutions.

The Directorate General of Export Development works to secure new export markets for Omani companies. From researching new export markets to advising on all aspects of market entry and development, it provides a comprehensive portfolio of services to clients. Moreover its international exhibition and matchmaking programmes ensure that Omani businesses have the opportunity to present their goods and services to potential customers.

OCIPED products

OCIPED produces a range of informative guides for its clients. These include:

- *Outlook Oman*: a quarterly newsletter.

- *Oman Trade Map*: a web-based guide to international markets.

- *Trade Secrets*: an export answer book for small and medium-sized exporters in Oman.

- *Oman Link*: contact details for its international representatives network.

- *Make our Exports your Advantage*: an export directory of Omani companies.

In addition, OCIPED produces information guides on investment opportunities and exports from Oman that are available in both hard-copy format and online at http://www.ociped.com
OCIPED can:

- provide project specific information;

- organize visits and meetings;

- assist investors in obtaining various government approvals;

- review project proposals prepared by investors and advise on appropriate entry strategies for setting up operations;

- provide forums for the private sector to advise on economic strategy;

- promote specific projects;

- assist local investors in identifying foreign partners through the network of OCIPED agents and other sources, and vice versa;

- carry out specific sector or project studies;

- participate in international exhibitions to promote Omani products in existing markets and open potential new markets;

- develop strategies for the enhancement of Omani exports;

- develop investment projects and promote Omani products through its international network of representatives;

- coordinate with regional and international organizations specialized in the field of export development to make use of their expertise for the development of Omani exports.

- disseminate to Omani companies, via e-mail, export enquiries obtained through the United Nations Trade Point Development Centre (UNTPDC).

Part 6

Establishing Trading Links with Oman

6.1

Living and Working in Oman

Val Kwaan

Almost the first thing that anyone who has visited the Sultanate of Oman will say about the experience is that the country is remarkably beautiful. To the north of Sur, a fertile coastal plain separates rugged mountains from the open Arabian Sea. In the hottest summer months in the Dhofar region, the south-west monsoon transforms the area around Salalah into a place of running waterfalls, rich green meadows and wandering cattle – unique in Arabia. In the central area lie the dramatic sands of the Wahibah desert. There is an astonishing diversity of scenery, climate and culture within the country, and although the pace of development since 1970 has been remarkably rapid, very little has been lost or spoilt. The people of Oman are very conservation conscious and caring of their environment and have made extraordinary efforts to lose nothing of value in the process of modernization.

In past centuries, the Sultanate of Oman was known as Muscat, Oman and Zanzibar – three separate and different countries drawn together by one ruler. This rich and ancient history is a very present force in modern life. To the visitor it will explain something of the diversity of languages and ethnic mix. Although Arabic is most frequently spoken, Swahili, Urdu and Hindi are all in common use. English is spoken widely, particularly in the cities. Oman, always the outward-looking, seafaring and trading nation, has absorbed people from all over the Indian Ocean region and remains very tolerant of foreign workers. For many people, the great ethnic diversity they encounter is one of the great pleasures of life, and this more than anything else makes the country a very comfortable place in which to live and work.

In Muscat and the other major cities, the enormous numbers of foreign workers and their families who have come and gone has geared the whole of society to fast and efficient ways of meeting, greeting and settling down. The larger companies often provide social support for their employees, but even those arriving knowing no one will find it easy to orientate. There are an enormous number of groups and societies dedicated either by language, country or interests, some of them publishing their own guide books for newcomers or arranging social events to put people who are a long way from their homes in touch with each other.

Travelling about in Oman means travelling by road. There is no rail system and public internal air travel is limited to flights from Muscat to Salalah and Muscat to Khasab in the Musandam Peninsula. The roads are mostly excellent and there is a well-developed and inexpensive public bus system serving all areas – local, long-distance and into the neighbouring United Arab Emirates. There is also a remarkable and very cheap bus system unique to Oman known as 'Baisa Buses'. These small orange and white vans, marked with their ministry licence numbers, are to be seen in large numbers everywhere. They will pull over for anyone who hails them, following their own chosen routes, the driver deviating for each passenger by arrangement. It has to be said, though, that a knowledge of Arabic, local geography and plenty of time are essential for this form of travel!

Licensed taxis are plentiful but relatively expensive, so it is also worth arguing the fare with the driver. Limousine services are to be found at the better hotels. They are clean and comfortable but again relatively expensive. Most people will opt to have their own private cars, as even within a city the distances to be covered each day are considerable and the extreme summer heat very demanding. Car prices and running costs are very reasonable, leasing or loan arrangements are easy to obtain, and this has inevitably led to considerable road congestion at peak times. Within Muscat, government ministries, oil companies and schools keep the same hours, which means that traffic is often heavy and sometimes dangerous. Although the police endeavour to enforce driving regulations, Oman has a poor road safety record. Short-term visitors may drive using their own licences or an international licence for up to one year, but holders of resident permits will require an Omani driving licence. In general, these can be obtained on production of a valid foreign licence or an international driving licence, but some nationalities will be required to take official lessons and a local test. For these reasons, some people may prefer to hire a driver.

Houses in Oman tend to be large, with expanses of tiled floors and many bathrooms to keep clean, but domestic help is inexpensive and many people opt for either full-time, often living-in staff, or part-time cleaning support. It is usually easy to arrange for full-time domestic staff to be sponsored through companies, mostly on two-year contracts.

In terms of housing: a reliable electricity supply is available to all but the most remote villages in the country, metered at the point of entry to your property, and at 240 volts. Clean but chlorinated water is piped to most houses or can be brought in by the tanker load, but it is recommended that bottled water is used for drinking. Rubbish is usually disposed of in large covered community bins, which are emptied daily. The system is efficient and the streets are generally kept very clean.

About 80 per cent of the population of Oman is under the age of 18. This startling statistic can be explained by the enormous amount of work carried out in the last 30 years in setting up a good, comprehensive health service, and has inevitably resulted in the need for a very well-developed education system. For the foreign worker, there is a rule that applies to most areas of domestic life: if what you need is also used by the Omanis themselves, then it will be good value; if it is peculiar to your own culture, then you will have to pay more. This is true for education, health care, food and everything you may need to buy.

The medium of instruction in the state school and university system is Arabic. However, within the larger cities, private schools exist to teach in many other languages to the standards of those countries. In Muscat, a number of schools provide the US high school diploma, the British GCSE and A-level systems, the Indian and Pakistani standards and the international baccalaureate diploma. Education costs in the private sector tend to be high, however.

The standard of medical practice within the state health system is generally high, but for those used to Western treatment it would be as well to take out private insurance. Most companies provide this for their staff. There are two private hospitals in Muscat and a large number of general and specialist private clinics in most towns. All but the most demanding treatments can be carried out within Oman and it is generally a very healthy place in which to live. The heat of summer must be respected, but the universal blessing of air-conditioning makes it possible to lead a normal life. There is very little risk from communicable disease, although malaria does occur. The beautiful climate of the winter months and the possibility of almost year-round outdoor recreation are particularly healthy for growing children.

Indeed, the climate makes possible a wealth of outdoor recreation. Many people buy 4WD vehicles in order to explore the vast and magnificent interior of the country, giving them access to camping, caving and mountain trekking. Oman has more than 1,700 kilometres of beach, almost all unspoiled and accessible. The Gulf of Oman is a whale sanctuary, several species of turtle lay their eggs on Omani beaches and the coral reefs provide superb diving opportunities. Within the capital area, there are several marinas and sailing clubs. All ball sports are to be found here, played with great seriousness and enthusiasm. There are a number of golf clubs where the game is played on 'browns', the golfer carrying his own square of AstroTurf around with him. The Automobile Club of Oman organizes a variety of motoring events and, quite remarkably, there is even an ice-skating rink in Muscat.

For the stay-at-home, most of the hotels have health clubs or spas, and some host concerts and plays given by visiting artists or local talent. Oman boasts the Royal Oman Symphony Orchestra, comprised wholly of Omani nationals, who give public concerts of a very high standard. There are a host of special interest groups, from the Oman Historical Society to cookery clubs and softball leagues, all putting on a variety of social events. As a result, life in Oman can be very busy!

There are a wide variety of restaurants in Muscat, and most other cities will at least have typical Arabian cafes. With regard to food shopping, the following rule-of-thumb applies: if you follow an Arabic or South Asian diet, food is cheap. Locally caught fish is remarkable in its variety and Oman grows much of its own fruit and vegetables. Everything else that you could want can be found, but sometimes at a price. There are many excellent, clean and well-stocked Western-style supermarkets, and the markets (or 'souks' as they are locally known) are fascinating in their rich variety. Imported goods do attract local tax and this is particularly high on pork products and alcohol, which are excluded from the Muslim diet. Bars are found in hotels and private clubs and alcohol may be brought for home consumption by non-Muslims from bonded warehouses, under a licensing system.

In many respects, Oman is a very special place. Its traditions are essentially democratic and open, the views of its people heard at all levels. Women play a full part in the country's life, not only in hospitals, shops and schools, but even as police officers and in government. The people are by nature quiet, dignified and very hospitable, and wherever you go, a smile will almost always be met with a smile, kindness and generous hospitality.

Oman is a safe place. There is, of course, some crime and thus sensible precautions should be taken, but little of it is more than petty. The country is very security conscious at all levels, justly proud of its smart armed services and the remarkable progress toward an affluent, modern society that it has made in so short a time. Almost everybody who comes to live and work in the Sultanate enjoys their time enormously, and when they leave it is with very happy memories.

Setting Up Agency and Distribution Agreements

James Harbridge and Nicholas Green,
Trowers & Hamlins, Muscat

Under Omani law it is not possible for a foreign entity to conduct business in the Sultanate without reference to a specific law. Therefore, if a foreign entity wishes to engage in any form of commercial activity in Oman, it must first find the relevant Omani law that permits it to carry out the type of commercial activities it is contemplating. If it wishes to ensure that its products are properly promoted, sold, marketed and distributed in Oman without the foreign entity actually being legally present in Oman undertaking those tasks itself, the applicable law will be the Commercial Agencies Law, Royal Decree 26/1977, as amended.

Definition

A 'commercial agent' is defined under the law as a merchant or company (legally registered in Oman) who enters into an agreement with a foreign manufacturer or supplier to sell, promote or distribute products or provide services in Oman as an agent. The term normally includes a distributor. A foreign principal's relationship with an agent duly registered with the Ministry of Commerce and Industry is governed by the Commercial Agencies Law. This law sets out certain requirements that must be fulfilled before an Omani entity can be appointed as an agent. If an individual, they must be an Omani citizen and ordinarily resident in Oman, not less than 18 years of age, and not guilty of any crimes. If a company, it should be registered in the Oman Commercial Register with its headquarters in Oman and the Omani shareholding should not be less than 51 per cent. The company's articles must permit it to import, trade and undertake commercial agency business.

Requirements

There are certain formalities relating to the contents of the agreement, which must be complied with, such as a precise description of the goods and services of the agency, the rights and obligations of the principal and agent, the term of the agency and the area that it covers. The agency contract should then be entered in the register maintained by the Ministry of Commerce and Industry.

In order for the Ministry of Commerce and Industry to accept the agreement, there must be collation of documentation, including a completed application form, signed and stamped by the agent; and the original authenticated agreement, together with a photocopy and a translation into Arabic. In addition to these documents, a copy of the Foreign Commercial and Investment Licence and a document from the agent confirming that no judgements that violate honour and good reputation have been recorded against him must be submitted. These documents must then be submitted to the Ministry of Commerce and Industry with the appropriate fee.

Once an agency agreement is in place, and if it is an exclusive agency, the foreign principal may not deal in Oman as regards the products in question other than through this agent, and if he does so, any commission that the agent would have generated from such dealings will be recoverable from the foreign principal.

Agent's duties

An agent is required by law to supply consumers with all the guarantees that are normally given by the original manufacturer or supplier, and must be in a position to provide spare parts where applicable and necessary workshops for repairs, unless the agent can submit evidence that spare parts and workshops are available with other agents or technicians in Oman. An agent is usually likely to request some 'comfort' in this regard from the foreign principal.

Principal's duties

Among other things, the principal is obliged to pay commission to the registered agent as and when earned by the agent, or if the principal sells his products or services directly in Oman or through an intermediary in contravention of the agency agreement.

Exclusivity

Until 1996, the Commercial Agencies Law provided that a foreign principal could only ever appoint one agent for any particular territorial area within Oman. However, this exclusivity requirement was removed in amendments to the law introduced in 1996, with the result that any number of agents can now be appointed in respect of the same products. Having said that, a foreign principal may well believe that it is beneficial to have an exclusive agent, and indeed agents will no doubt continue to hold out for an exclusive agency, although their ability to do so will, of course, depend upon the balance of bargaining power as between the agent and the foreign principal.

Abuse of right

While agents should register their agency agreements, they sometimes fail to do so, or they fail to renew registration certificates. An Omani agent could lose the benefit of the protective legislation provisions detailed in the Commercial Agencies Law if the agreement is unregistered. Article 11(d) of the Commercial Agencies Law states that a claim for 'abuse of right' (as detailed below) will not be heard if it relates to an unregistered agency. A registered agent can, however, claim compensation if he can prove an 'abuse of right' by a foreign principal.

Article 10 of the Commercial Agencies Law gives examples of such 'abuses' and, in essence, an 'abuse of right' constitutes a termination of an agency agreement without a material breach by the agent of the agreement to justify that termination, or a failure by a foreign principal to renew a fixed-term agency agreement upon expiry. Therefore, it is wise to note that a principal, seeking to avoid any need to pay out compensation, cannot fail to renew an agent's contract without proof of a material breach of contract on the part of the agent. The right of a registered agent to claim compensation is therefore something that a foreign principal must bear in mind. Compensation for an 'abuse of right' could equate to three years' net profits derived by the agent from the agency business in question. An agent may also receive compensation for any capital expenditure he has incurred solely in relation to the agency in question.

Other effects

Oman does recognize and implement the concept of 'contractual freedom'. Therefore, a foreign principal in a contractual relationship with an Omani agent can terminate that relationship, although of course there is the risk of compensation having to be paid to the agent as per the 'abuse of right' legislation.

It now appears to be the practice of the Ministry of Commerce and Industry to register willingly a foreign principal's relationship with a new agent notwithstanding the existence of a dispute between the principal and the former agent. While the Commercial Agencies Law allows the former agent to apply for a ban on the importation of the principal's goods, the author has never known this sanction to be applied by the Minister of Commerce and Industry.

Contracting out of compensation

The question is often asked as to whether there are any ways in which the agent can be persuaded to agree that a claim for compensation will not be advanced in the event of termination of the agreement. Such a clause would simply be disregarded if the matter came before the courts. However, if there is a clause in the agency agreement that requires matters to be referred to arbitration, the courts will normally uphold this clause, even if the arbitration is to be conducted abroad and is subject to foreign law. A foreign law and arbitration clause has therefore often been used as a tactic by foreign principals to discourage an agent from claiming compensation upon the termination of an agency agreement, but if the agent is determined to pursue his claim, and is prepared to first exhaust the arbitration route, he may then be entitled to return to the courts in Oman if, in that foreign arbitration, he was not awarded compensation that he would have been entitled to receive had the matter been dealt with in Oman in the first place with Omani law as the applicable law. However, it is uncertain whether the Omani courts would accept jurisdiction in such circumstances – hence the use of the word 'may'.

Another option that foreign principals often suggest is that they simply agree with the agent not to register the agency agreement with the Ministry of Commerce and Industry, as the Commercial Agencies Law – and therefore the right to compensation – applies only to registered agreements. It cannot be denied that parties do operate on this basis in Oman, but the fact is that it is contrary to the law for the agent to act as an agent without a registered agreement in place, and it is contrary to the law for a foreign principal to do business in Oman without a registered agent.

In essence, most foreign principals only encounter serious difficulties with their agents when the agreement between them is terminated. As stated above, in contrast to the often-held belief that Omani law 'ties you to an agent for life', it must be pointed out that the agency agreement can always be terminated. Compensation will only be awarded if there were no reasonable grounds for termination. If the registered agent is under-performing, that should relieve a principal of the obligation to pay compensation, always provided that the evidential position is solid. In truth, the courts award compensation, not a penalty, and compensation should therefore only be payable where it is just, bearing in mind the agent's conduct, that he should be compensated for what he would have rightfully expected to receive from the agency relationship in the immediate upcoming years. Nonetheless, the whole issue of 'abuse of rights' is one upon which foreign principals should seek specialist legal advice before executing any agency contract with an Oman entity.

6.3

Practical Guidelines for Doing Business in Oman

*Sean Angle and Nicholas Green, Trowers &
Hamlins, Muscat*

Introduction

This chapter seeks to provide a series of practical pointers for those
considering doing business in the Sultanate of Oman. It will briefly cover
topics such as the investment environment, taxation and Omanization,
and will endeavour to offer an insight into some of the regulatory
requirements of which foreign investors should be aware when considering setting up an Omani presence.

Business and investment environment

In common with other countries in the Middle East, Oman is rich in
natural mineral and other resources. Indeed, oil has been the driving
force of the Omani economy since the Sultanate began commercial
production in 1967. The oil industry was initially responsible for the
financing of the modern Oman and continues to support the country's
high standard of living today. Practically none of its modern and
expansive infrastructure, including electrical utilities, telephone services, roads, public education and medical services would be available
today without the influence of this 'black gold' and the Sultanate's other
major natural resources. In addition to extensive oil reserves, Oman
has substantial natural gas reserves, which are expected to play a
leading role in the Omani economy in the 21st Century.

To reduce Oman's dependence on oil, the government's latest Five-
Year Development Plan is aimed at encouraging private-sector diversifi-
cation into other industries. Approximately 60 per cent of the country's
GDP is now generated outside the oil and gas sector, as compared to 33
per cent in 1975 when the First Plan was implemented. Oman's Sixth
Five-Year Development Plan (2001–2005) contains the policy of promot-

ing private-sector investment into non-oil and non-gas industrial activities. For foreign investors, investment opportunities are available in priority areas targeted for development by the government, including agriculture, fishing, light industrial production, public utility projects and tourism. The government particularly encourages industrial production that is export-oriented or which will replace imported products.

Investment incentives

The Organization and Encouragement of Industry Law, Royal Decree 1/1979, is one of a raft of laws governing the provision of incentives to foreign investors in Oman. The law established the Industrial Development Committee, which seeks to promote increased productivity and efficiency, as well as the development and consolidation of industrial installations. Proposals qualify for incentives only if Omani nationals make up 25 per cent of their total workforce, unless the Ministry of Commerce and Industry specifically rules otherwise.

Investment incentives include the provision of industrial plots in industrial zones for nominal charges; preference in the allocation of government land; interest-free or subsidized loans with long payment terms; reduced charges for water, electricity and fuel; financial assistance for the development of economic and technical feasibility studies; and the expedited arrangement of immigration visas and permits for foreign workers.

Tax exemptions

Tax exemptions from corporate tax and customs duty may be granted by the Ministry of Finance. Tax exemptions are available for entities engaging in manufacturing, mining, agriculture, fishing, fish processing, animal breeding, tourism, the export of manufactured and reprocessed products, higher education and public utilities. Exemptions are granted for five-year periods effective from the date at which production begins or services are first rendered; a five-year extension may be granted. Management agreements and construction contracts do not qualify for tax exemptions.

Companies engaged in the activities listed above may also obtain an exemption from the payment of customs duty on exports and on imports of equipment, spare parts and raw materials.

Taxation

There is no personal income tax in Oman. Tax is applied solely to companies and establishments in the Sultanate, and for that to occur it is not even necessary to be registered for tax. The requirement is for a 'permanent establishment' to exist and for income to arise in Oman. The tax authorities interpret this criterion very widely to include, for example, the entire income of a procurement contract performed by a foreign contractor where commissioning takes place in Oman, even if such part of the contract is of minimal value.

The tax charge is against income, from all sources, which has been realized or has arisen in the country. All deductions, such as business costs or depreciation, must be justified as an allowable deduction in terms of the tax legislation. Permitted depreciation rates are set out in this legislation. In practice, the allowable deductions mean that tax is charged on what is substantially a profit calculation, but it is important to appreciate the underlying basis of the system.

Royal Decrees 68/2000 and 69/2000 have amended certain provisions of the Law of Income Tax on Companies, Royal Decree 47/1981, and Law of Profit Tax on Commercial and Industrial Establishments, Royal Decree 77/1989, respectively. The changes have been made consistent with the government's initiative to attract foreign investment and introduce major reforms to its existing legislation. A summary of the recent changes made to the tax laws in Oman is set out below:

- The maximum tax rate applicable to branches of foreign companies has been reduced from 50 per cent to 30 per cent from tax year 2001.

- Mixed companies with a foreign participation of up to 70 per cent will be taxable, on taxable income earned above RO30,000, at a single rate of 12 per cent from tax year 2001. Previously, this rate of tax was available only if the foreign participation did not exceed 49 per cent.

- Mixed companies with a foreign participation of more than 70 per cent will be taxable at rates applicable to branches of foreign companies, maximum tax rate of 30 per cent, from tax year 2001.

- Shipping companies (both Omani-registered and foreign) are exempt from taxation.

- Dividend income is no longer taxable irrespective of the tax status of the investee company as from tax year 2000.

- Professional establishments owned by individual natural persons are taxable as from this tax year.

Withholding tax

For foreign companies that do not have a permanent establishment in Oman and charge a) 'itawat',[1] b) fees in return for management, c) rent for equipment or machinery, or d) money charged in return for the transfer of technical expertise or for research and development from companies or permanent establishments existing in Oman, a 10 per cent rate of tax is applied. This tax is levied on the gross income received by the foreign company and is an exception from the tax rates and the provisions mentioned above.

The local establishment or company which pays any of the 'itawat', fees, rents or amounts of money mentioned in the previous paragraph is itself responsible for the deduction of the tax from its payment to the foreign company and its accounting to the tax authorities.

Annual requirements for corporations

Registration fees

All business entities operating in Oman must periodically pay registration fees to the Ministry of Commerce and Industry. The amount of the fees and the frequency of their payment depend on the type of business entity. For example, Omani-registered companies pay an initial fee of RO1.5 for each RO1,000 of share capital, and an annual renewal fee ranging from RO20 to RO200. Annual fees must also be paid to the Oman Chamber of Commerce and Industry (OCCI). Each entity must apply annually for a renewal of its OCCI certificate and the fees range from RO25 to RO625, depending on the classification of the business entity.

Audit

Taxable entities of a certain size must undergo annual audits to produce the financial statements that accompany their annual income tax returns. Certain larger entities must also perform statutory audits.

Annual shareholders' meeting

All joint-stock companies must hold annual shareholders' meetings within four months after the end of their financial year. Limited liability companies (LLCs) must hold annual shareholders' meetings within six months after the end of their financial year.

---

[1] The Arabic word 'itawat' is often translated as 'lump sums' but is sometimes also translated as 'royalties' as it denotes a payment in return for the use or benefit of something. In the particular decree at issue here, the word is used to denote any one-off payment or series of payments made in return for the use or benefit of another's property (including incorporeal property such as intellectual property rights).

Tax filing

All business organizations, including those wholly owned by Omani nationals, must file provisional and annual income tax returns.

Legal reserves

Both joint-stock companies and LLCs must set aside 10 per cent of their net profits as a legal reserve annually until the reserve reaches one-third of the company's capital (Commercial Companies Law (CCL), Articles 106 and 154). This reserve is never made available for distribution to shareholders.

Omanization

Omanization has steadily become more of a central plank in the government's development plans for the Sultanate. The aim of Omanization is to limit the Sultanate's dependence on expatriate staff. Non-Omanis are not permitted to work in Oman unless clearance has been obtained from the Ministry of Social Affairs, Labour and Vocational Training. Royal Decree 11/1999 states that employers must employ Omanis wherever possible, and for each non-Omani employed an employer must make an annual contribution of RO100 towards a vocational training levy. Different sectors of industry are given different Omanization percentages, which must be met. These range from 15 per cent (contracting) to 60 per cent (transport, storage and communications). Failure to reach industry targets results in a liability to pay fines.

Ministerial Decision 298/2000 provided that Gulf Cooperation Council (GCC) nationals working in Oman are to be considered as part of the relevant Omanization percentage calculation in the workforces of private-sector establishments. GCC nationals must be given priority in employment after Omani nationals, and efforts must be made to treat GCC nationals at a par with Omani nationals in respect of benefits and job entitlements. The government prescribes a minimum monthly wage of RO100 for Omani employees, in addition to which employers must pay their Omani employees a monthly accommodation allowance of RO10 and a monthly transportation allowance of RO10.

Conclusion

The above guidelines on doing business in Oman were selected for their relevance to those thinking of the practical issues involved in running a business in the Sultanate. None of the information provided above, however, should be regarded as a substitute for up-to-date and comprehensive professional advice.

6.4

WTO Membership

Dr Hamed H Al Dhahab, Director-General of Industry, Ministry of Commerce and Industry, Ruwi

The Sultanate of Oman's accession to the World Trade Organization (WTO) in November 2000 necessitated making concessions and commitments on goods, specific commitments on services, commitments on domestic support and export subsidies to agriculture, as well as the enactment of new, or the revision of existing, legislation to bring it into conformity with the provisions of the WTO.

In the schedule of concessions and commitments on goods, Oman has bound customs import duties on all agricultural and industrial goods. On a majority of agricultural products, the Oman has bound duties at 15 per cent, with a few exceptions in respect to sensitive agricultural products, where Oman has succeeded in binding duties at fairly high rates, thus providing adequate protection to local producers. Examples include: liquid milk, which has been bound at 75 per cent; eggs at 75 per cent in season and 20 per cent out of season; fruit and vegetables (only those grown in Oman) at 80 per cent in season and 30 per cent out of season; and bananas at 100 per cent. The implication here is that Oman can levy customs duties up to the level of the bound rates if necessary, but cannot go beyond these under normal circumstances.

Similarly, with industrial products where Oman has bound customs duties on a majority of items at 15 per cent, the bound rates are higher than the currently applied rates, thus allowing the country the freedom to provide protection to existing or future domestic industries, if necessary. In a few cases where the bound rates are equal to or lower than the currently applied rates, Oman has succeeded in negotiating a transitional period of at least five years that will give domestic industries a reasonable time during which to prepare for competing with imported products. Examples would include chemicals at 0 per cent, 5.5 per cent, 6.5 per cent (to become effective after five years for most chemicals and

10 years for plastics), and Information Technology Agreement (ITA) products at 0 per cent (effective after five years).

Oman views duty-free entry of ITA products to be in the long-term interest of the Sultanate, as cheaper such products will have a positive impact on the Omani economy. Low duties on chemicals will also be beneficial to Oman. Considering that Oman has a comparative advantage in petrochemicals, it is in no need for high-duty protection in this sector. In addition, Oman's potential exports of petrochemicals will have easy access to developed countries' markets and to those developing countries that have reduced their tariffs to very low levels.

The most significant challenge of globalization as a result of Oman's accession to the WTO, however, will be felt in the service sector as a result of foreign competition. Oman views services trade liberalization as a vehicle through which to attract efficient and competitive foreign service suppliers to invest and bring their technology and expertise into the Sultanate as this will benefit the rest of the national economy and fit eminently with the national policy of economic diversification. Oman, however, did not want to compromise its twin objectives of Omanization in ownership and Omanization in personnel in the course of services trade liberalization and so it has managed to safeguard its position by placing limitations on foreign equity and the number of foreign personnel that foreign suppliers can bring in from abroad.

During negotiations on trade in services for WTO accession, Oman agreed to raise the ceiling of foreign participation from 49 per cent to 70 per cent, effective from 1 January 2001, except for a number of sensitive sub-sectors where foreign equity is limited to a lower level – such as motion picture and videotape distribution services (49 per cent); cinema ownership and operation (51 per cent); restaurants (49 per cent); selling and marketing of air transportation services (51 per cent); computer reservation services for air travel (51 per cent); storage and warehouse services (51 per cent); and janitorial and packing services (51 per cent). However, Oman has agreed to allow either branch offices or wholly foreign-owned subsidiaries in six sectors: in computer-related services (wholly foreign-owned subsidiaries from beginning of 2003); courier services (wholly foreign-owned subsidiaries from beginning of 2003); telecommunications services (wholly foreign-owned subsidiaries from 2005); banking services (wholly foreign-owned subsidiaries from beginning of 2003, branches of foreign banks continuing to be allowed); insurance services (branches of foreign companies as well as foreign-owned companies from the beginning of 2003); and other financial services (wholly foreign-owned subsidiaries from date of accession to the WTO, 9 November 2000). Oman hopes that this further liberalization will increase the flow of foreign investment and transfer of technology and modern know-how into the country.

Oman has placed in its service commitments a 20 per cent limitation on the foreign personnel that foreign service companies wishing to establish a presence in Oman can bring from abroad for each company. The liberalization of the services sector would engender growth of this sector, which would in turn create additional jobs. The additional growth would more than compensate for the jobs that could be taken up by the foreigners under the 20 per cent commitment.

In the process of WTO accession, Oman has also enacted new laws and regulations and revised existing laws to bring them into conformity with the provisions of the WTO agreements. The most important laws enacted by Oman are the Customs Valuation Law and the various laws for the protection of intellectual property rights in the field of patents, industrial designs, plant varieties, geographical indications and layout design of integrated circuits. The existing laws on copyrights and trademarks were also revised to make them TRIPS consistent. Other legislations issued were in the field of standards and phyto-sanitary measures to align the procedures with the WTO agreements on Technical Barriers to Trade (TBT) and Sanitary and Phyto-Sanitary (SPS) measures. Oman has also removed bans and quotas on imports of eggs, milk, fruit and vegetables and replaced them with tariffs, since bans and quotas on the import of agricultural products are not permissible under WTO rules.

Oman's WTO accession entails only limited obligations, in view of the fact that the country's market is already open. Oman has not undertaken substantive commitments in its WTO accession that are inconsistent with its own autonomous policies. Oman therefore has nothing to lose and much to gain from WTO accession and globalization. Oman views globalization, contrary to the perceptions of some people, as generally a force for growth and prosperity, as has been witnessed during the last two decades when living standards of many countries around the globe have risen as trade barriers came down rapidly and markets of different countries became increasingly open. Trade is the primary vehicle through which the benefits of globalization are realized, and the liberalization that Oman has committed itself to undertake in the services sector – particularly in the important sectors of finance and telecommunications – will further increase the efficiency of these sectors as well as other sectors such as tourism and the manufacturing sector, thus assisting them to compete both domestically and in world markets.

The Law of Income Tax on Companies was amended by Royal Decree 69/2000, issued on 12 August 2000, streamlining the income tax on company profits and providing non-discriminatory treatment between 100 per cent Omani-owned companies and joint-stock companies, irrespective of the extent of foreign capital participation in them, and even non-joint stock companies in which foreign capital participation is 70 per cent or less. Such companies will be taxed at 12 per cent on profits exceeding the exemption limit of the first RO30,000 (US$77,400). Corporate rate tax for 100 per cent foreign companies, mixed companies where foreign share-holding is more than 70 per cent and proprietorships owned by foreign individuals will be taxed on the highest band of profit (more than RO100,000 (US$258,000)) at the rate of 30 per cent, whereas earlier the rate of tax on the highest band was 50 per cent. These are perceived to be very favourable and attractive features of Oman's tax regime.

Moreover, profits of companies engaged in the following areas are exempt from taxation for a period of five years, which exemption could be renewed once for another period of five years:

- manufacturing industries;

- export of locally manufactured or processed products;

- promotion of tourism;

- agricultural production;

- processing and manufacture of animal products;

- agricultural industries;

- fishing industry and fish processing;

- utilization and provision of services such as the public utilities projects.

Salalah Port and Free Zone

Salalah Port Services Company (SPS), Muscat

Salalah port

Long known throughout the ancient Arab world for its trade in frankincense, Salalah, the capital of the Dhofar region in southern Oman, is once again establishing itself as an important port for the international maritime trade. Four hundred years ago, Omani ships sailed the high seas to China, India, Africa and the Red Sea. The port is seen as a natural sequence to past glory as the Indian Ocean rim area, and in particular the Gulf and Indian Sub-Continent, allows coverage of a large area with over 1.6 billion consumers from a single location, saving approximately 3.5 days over other Arabian Gulf ports.

Oman is the second largest country in the Arabian Gulf, with a coastline stretching 1,700 kilometres from the Straits of Hormuz to the border with Yemen. Since the accession of HM Sultan Qaboos in 1970, the economy has grown dramatically. The heavy reliance on oil is being reduced in phased projects aimed at diversifying the economy into non-oil sectors and shifting investment from the public to the private sector. One of the largest of these projects is Salalah port. One of the most endearing aspects of Oman is that it seems to have balanced the advantages of the technological age against the need to preserve the strong cultural, traditional and spiritual values that characterize its people. True progress is development without the destruction of all that is good within a community or nation. The government of Oman has clearly focused its efforts on improving the lives of its people without destroying the country's unique culture, human values, or respect for the environment. When one looks at modern Oman and the considerable achievements that have taken place during the rule of HM Sultan Qaboos, one must also recognize the national priorities that have guided the decisions behind the remarkable growth that has occurred over the past two and a half decades.

The Omani government owns Salalah port and has given a 30-year concession to Salalah Port Services Company (SPS) to manage and operate the facility. SPS was formed as an Omani public joint-stock company (SAOG) with a 70 per cent local shareholding and 30 per cent equity held by Maersk Line of Denmark. SPS was incorporated on 15 September 1997 and commenced commercial operations on 1 November 1998. SPS is engaged in leasing, equipping, operating and managing the container terminal and conventional port facility at Salalah port. SPS holds the concession for operating and managing this world-class container hub port and is the project manager for the proposed Salalah Port Free Zone. SPS is also the port authority on behalf of the government, thus making it one of the world's few fully privatized port facilities.

The vision of the port was to build a world-class container terminal that would have a positive effect on the economy, employment rate and tourism of the country and to also position Oman to become a global trading partner. The speed at which the project developed was extraordinary. From the signing of a contract to build the terminal in December 1996 and construction starting in April 1997, a world-class container terminal with state-of-the-art equipment was opened in November 1998 with two completed berths. Two further berths were delivered three months ahead of schedule in April 1999. It is the only Middle East port, and one of the very few ports in the world, able to accept the huge S-class vessels, in addition to which it has one of the highest productivity levels anywhere in the world.

Salalah port is located 25 kilometres south of Salalah city. It is a deepwater port and can accommodate large vessels up to 15 metres draft. The container terminal has four berths totalling 1,236 metres in length with a depth of 16 metres. The terminal has a nominal capacity of 2.2 million TEUs a year. The dockside facilities include 11 high-speed, 66-tonne capacity cranes designed to load ships up to 22 containers wide. The port has 22 rubber-tyred gantries and four top-loaders. There are facilities for 500 reefer containers. The General Cargo Terminal has 11 berths ranging in length from 115 metres to 600 metres with a draft of from 3 metres to 16 metres and a dedicated oil pier. In February 2002, BP Marine and SPS concluded a bunker fuel supply agreement. Refuelling operations began in February. The location of Salalah along the main east–west shipping routes makes it a strategic port of call for the world's container vessels. With world-class facilities and unmatched productivity already available to them, the addition of bunkering services will provide vessels with the ability to refuel during their journey, thereby allowing them to carry additional cargo. BP Marine has chartered a 35,000-tonne tanker and two refuelling barges according to its exacting specifications to ensure maximum safety and efficiency for the service.

In only three full years of operation, Salalah port can boast having broken the world record twice for the number of container moves achieved per hour. Its impressive productivity records, which are well above and in some cases more than twice as high as other regional ports, coupled with its state-of-the-art equipment, make Salalah port *the* port of the future and lay the foundation for success in reaching its goal of becoming one of the six global trans-shipment hubs.

Proposed Free Trade Zone

Salalah: global trans-shipment and logistics hub

Salalah port is positioning itself as one of the world's six global trans-shipment hubs. This will now be further enhanced by the development of the Salalah Free Trade Zone, a world-class facility owned by a public-private partnership between the Omani government, SPS and Hillwood. Hillwood is a US-based real estate development and investment firm with a proven track record in delivery of world-class, master-planned real estate projects, products and services.

Designed to attract transportation, logistics and consumer product companies and their real estate-related operations, the strategic location of Salalah port will allow these companies to achieve business- and transportation-related efficiencies in regional and international markets. In addition, the business incentives available in the Salalah Free Trade Zone will allow these businesses to add value to their products and achieve efficiencies in both operations and delivery times, thus making their business more profitable.

A master-planned community of the future

The Salalah Free Trade Zone is a master-planned community of approximately 2,400 hectares (6,000 acres), which will be developed in multiple phases. It will offer a mix of industrial, light manufacturing, freight station, distribution, research and development, commercial office, retail, resort, hotel and housing products. Phase I will provide customers with approximately 510,000 square metres (5.4 million square feet) of container freight station, distribution, retail, residential and light manufacturing facilities. It is anticipated that Phase I will create over 3,000 direct jobs.

In addition, Salalah Free Trade Zone will provide its customers with access to the finest and most complete communications and IT systems in the world. Broadband fibre-optic infrastructure for voice, data and video will be provided throughout the project area.

World-class incentives to complement a world-class project

The following incentives are in the process of being developed and will be provided in the Salalah Free Trade Zone:

- 100 per cent foreign ownership of Free Trade Zone companies.
- All import and export of goods will be free from customs duties.
- No minimum capital requirements for Free Trade Zone companies.
- No taxes on profits or dividends of Free Trade Zone companies.
- No taxes on the personal income of Free Trade Zone employees.
- No restrictions on repatriation of capital, profits and investments.
- Omanization requirements of only 10 per cent.
- Free Trade Zone companies will have the ability to participate in existing export guarantee arrangements provided to other Omani companies by Omani financial institutions.
- 'One-stop shop' for licences, permits, visas and customs clearance.
- Flexible customs procedures.

Best in design and development standards

The Salalah Free Trade Zone will offer customers the finest-quality industrial and manufacturing facilities in a master-planned community. Institutional quality design guidelines, including landscaping and signage programmes, will be instituted for all development within the project. These guidelines will ensure that the customers' commitment and investment are protected. International building standards will be used and all customers will be required to maintain strict adherence to international hazardous materials guidelines.

Complete flexibility in site selection and construction support

The Salalah Free Trade Zone can accommodate virtually any type and size of facility and the owners will customize the standard building type to suit customers' needs. Customers will be able to choose from:

- land on a long-term ground lease basis to construct their own building;
- occupancy in pre-built speculative buildings;
- having their facility 'built to suit' by the Free Trade Zone company.

The Salalah Free Trade Zone has the ability to provide all necessary development, design and construction services and their respective permits and approvals, in addition to logistics, communications, IT, furnishing and management services.

A 'one-stop shop' facility will be available on site and online for tenants, customers and employers, in which numerous services will be offered, including:

- assistance with all necessary licensing with Omani authorities;

- all visas and immigration services, health cards, drivers' licences, car registration services;

- help with international accounting, consultancy, local law firms, banks;

- on-site accommodation for customers and their employees;

- recruitment agency for employment of skilled local workforce;

- business-friendly, result-driven management team.

Services include:

- logistics (freight handling, storage, shipping related, brokerage, transport);

- Free Trade Zone administration: customs-related processing (activation, service, monitoring, inventory control);

- marketing (brokerage, leasing and sales);

- licences and permits (visas, work permits, construction permits, utility connections);

- sponsorship;

- development (development and construction management, infrastructure and facilities);

- property management;

- energy management;

- technology (equipment, service, processing);

- air-sea transport/fulfilment.

Part 7

Marketing in Oman

Shell in Oman: Marketing Case Study

Nicholas Pattison, Managing Director, and Faisal AlHashar, Corporate Affairs and Business Development Manager, Shell Oman Marketing Company, Oman

The Royal Dutch/Shell Group grew out of an alliance made in 1907 between Royal Dutch Petroleum Company and the Shell Transport and Trading Company plc, by which the two companies agreed to merge while keeping their separate identities. Today, Shell companies form one of the world's largest businesses.

In the Sultanate of Oman, the Group witnessed the birth of Oman's renaissance and had the opportunity to be an active participant in its development from the country's initial discovery of oil through the Group's association and partnership with the Omani government in Petroleum Development of Oman (PDO), where Shell owns 34 per cent of the equity to the present day.

In the fuel marketing business in Oman, the Shell Group was granted trading rights in 1958. As Shell SEA, the forerunner to Shell Markets (Oman) LLC, it operated through a locally appointed agent. Its retail operation started at a time when there was minimum infrastructure in the country and cars were few. Drums of fuel were brought to Omani shores by ship, transported to small, locally made wooden boats, rolled onto the beach and transported to their storage destination for distribution. The market for petroleum products was very small, with the only major consumers being the armed forces and an oil prospecting company.

With the accession in 1970 of His Majesty Sultan Qaboos, Oman began a process of rapid modernization. In that year, a marketing franchise was granted to Shell for its retail business, which started operations as Shell Markets (Oman).

The development, manufacture and marketing of fuels and lubricants is a highly specialized business, and one in which Shell is recognized as a world leader. In Oman, the businesses have developed to their current strong position in all sectors of the fuel marketing business: retail fuel sales to the public via dealer-owned filling stations; direct fuel sales to government and commercial entities and users of aviation fuel; and non-fuel sales of lubricants and greases.

In 1984, the Shell Group set up a joint venture with local partners to blend lubricants in Oman. Oman Lubricants Company was formed with a 45 per cent local shareholding, with the balance held by companies of the Shell Group. A lubricants blending plant was constructed in 1985 at Mina al Fahal on land leased from the government and operations commenced fully in 1986. The subsequent success of Oman Lubricants Company can be attributed to two key areas: first, the plant, which was designed and built using the expertise of the Shell Group specialists, has proven to be reliable and flexible; second, Oman Lubricants Company has had access to the Shell brand and international formulations and has been able to sell its products through Shell Markets (Oman) facilities and network and exported through other Shell Group companies outside Oman.

In January 1996, as a gift to the Sultanate on its 25th National Day anniversary, Shell International Group initiated the 'Intilaaqah' programme, with funding initially for five years, which since then has been further renewed annually. This project, as well as being of help to young Omanis – the country's main asset – would contribute to the development and diversification of the country's economy and demonstrate the commitment of Shell to the Sultanate.

In line with government policy, training is conducted in both Arabic and English in qualified institutes that are approved to deliver Intilaaqah's training to NVQ 2 and 3 in business planning and ownership. During training, trainees will learn how to prepare a full business plan and part of this plan will be a feasibility study of their own business idea, based on practical market research. To date, the programme has benefited more than 390 graduates, of whom 75 have started their own businesses and some provide employment to other Omanis.

Today, the Intilaaqah programme is recognized among the best private-sector initiatives for diversification and Omanization. With this in mind, the government recently launched the 'Sanad' (Support) programme, aimed at providing soft loans to young entrepreneurs to help them start their own businesses – a challenge which previously faced many young Omanis who needed capital to start their dream project after their successful graduation from the Intilaaqah programme.

With the formation of the Muscat Securities Market (MSM), the Omani government started to implement various incentives to encourage the flotation of privately owned companies. This process was seen as a tool to get more Omanis to benefit from the opportunities derived from the projects in the development of the needed infrastructure in Oman.

While Shell Markets (Oman) and its joint venture subsidiaries continued to achieve impressive financial results, with more than RO136 million in turnover and RO4.4 million in profits in 1996, the Shell Group decided to float the company, thus making it the first foreign company in Oman to be floated on the MSM.

Accordingly, Shell Oman Marketing Company was formed in August 1997 as an Omani public joint-stock company (SAOG). The response was overwhelming, where the initial public offering (IPO) of 40 per cent was 32 times oversubscribed, which required the Ministry of Commerce and Industry to create a special methodology for the allocation of shares. Today, there are more than 7,000 shareholders in Shell Oman Marketing Company, representing a wide spectrum of the economy, from financial institutions and pension funds to small investors.

Today, Shell Oman Marketing Company operates 117 retail fuel stations, 31 Select shops and employs a staff of around 230, over 70 per cent of whom are Omani, giving vital in-depth knowledge of local activities, practices and practical needs. Since its formation as a joint-stock company, Shell Oman Marketing Company has been delivering strong dividends to its shareholders and maximizing its shareholders' long-term value. In October 2001, the share price averaged approximately RO6.200, placing Shell Oman among the top companies based on share price and among the top five in market capitalization.

In 2000, the company's revenue reached RO145 million with a net profit of RO7.890 million, which led the board to approve a dividend of RO0.650 per share. Some Shell Oman shareholders, in coordination with the Capital Market Authority (CMA) and MSM, received their dividends by direct electronic transfer to their bank accounts, once again making Shell Oman the first company in the country to transfer dividends electronically.

In both 1999 and 2000, Shell Oman ranked number one in a survey of Oman's largest companies conducted by the *Oman Economic Review*, a local business magazine; the company was also voted number one in a survey of best practices published in January 2001 by *Business Today*, another leading publication in the Sultanate.

Across Oman, customers' needs are changing and Shell Oman Marketing is determined to anticipate and respond quickly to these evolving market conditions. To this end, Shell service stations have continually evolved, as can be witnessed in the rapid expansion of Select – Oman's first 24-hour convenience store. Other innovations include the introduction of Shell Cards – the Sultanate's first electronic fuel payment system for commercial customers – and a trial launch of Shell Genie – a new and innovative way of changing motor oil that is clean, convenient and environmentally friendly.

Health, safety and the environment (HSE) are among the primary concerns and the focus of attention in all areas of the company's operations. Since its formation, Shell Oman Marketing Company has focused its attention on maintaining high environmental standards, the generation of profit and the support of social initiatives under what is termed in Shell the 'Sustainable Development Framework'.

This focus on the environment has developed and progressed in Shell Oman in line with local and international principles. The company follows strict international standards to ensure that the company applies the latest techniques in environmental management. This is achieved by adopting both administrative and technical tools to assist in avoiding any harmful effect to the environment. This stratagem is derived from the fact that the protection of the environment cannot be achieved through internal legislation and policies and by activities associated with the clean-up after an environmental disaster, but rather through the elimination or reduction of any impact by company operations to the environment. Environmental risk management-based techniques are therefore part of the armoury of tools used to ensure that capital spend is optimized in relation to environmental hazards.

In 2000, the company participated in a number of Shell initiatives to explore ways of introducing e-enabled services to its customers. In October 2000, the Shell Oman website (http://www.shelloman.com) was launched, making Shell Oman the first Shell company in the Middle East and South Asia to have its own website. The site is intended not only to be interesting and informative, but also to give customers a forum in which they can communicate directly and easily with the company. Customers can, for example, order fuel cards and see their balances online. At the end of 2001, a system that allows the ordering of other products over the Internet went under trial, which, if successful, will become a permanent feature.

Periodically, and in association with other Shell companies in the region, Shell Oman conducts research to measure its reputation among key publics in Oman, which is then compared to Shell's reputation in other parts of the world. In 2000, MORI research revealed that Shell Oman had a strong reputation, with 82 per cent favourability in that year versus 56 per cent in 1997.

In addition to this research, Shell Oman regularly engages in discussions with its stakeholders to address how strategies and operational matters can either be devised or altered to provide social, environmental and economic benefit. This is the process upon which the company's operations are regularly scrutinized to meet stakeholders' expectations. Such a policy is derived from Shell's commitment to the nation and its desire for a long association and partnership in a sustainable environment in Oman.

7.2

Media and Advertising

*Radha Mukherjee, General Manager, OHI
DDB Advertising & Publicity Company,
Muscat*

The media represent perhaps the most eloquent introduction to any country. A first-time visitor gets a first-hand feel of the country the moment he opens the morning's paper. The editorial content, width and depth of coverage, and at a more basic level the look and print quality, together create a total impression of any country – the level of development, technology, press freedom, political leanings, value systems and a great deal more. The volume of advertising too, while contributing directly to the financial wellbeing of the media, is also a reflection of the state of the market, the level of competition, the marketing and creative talent in the country, and so forth. The Sultanate of Oman, as a comparatively young country, can be proud of its media of an overall high quality, particularly so with respect to the print medium.

Press

Press is the dominant medium in the country. Oman has five daily newspapers that comprehensively cover local and international news. Three of these are Arabic: *Al Watan, Al Shabiba* and the *Oman Daily*. The latter is government-owned, as is the *Oman Daily Observer*, its sister paper produced in English. The other English newspaper is the *Times of Oman*, a private newspaper that is particularly popular with the large Asian expatriate community in the country. This is reflected in its slant towards wider coverage of news of the Asian Sub-Continent. *Al Shabiba* is published by the same group and tends to focus on the youth of the country, as is, in fact, suggested by its name.

In the absence of audited circulation figures, or certified readership data, it is hard to tell which one is the leader. Each has its own loyal clientele. In terms of quality, they are all of a uniformly high standard. A quirk of this market until a few years ago was the non-publication of newspapers on Friday, the weekly holiday. While today all newspapers bring out a Friday paper, the fewer advertisements are perhaps an indication that advertisers do not believe there to be much weekend readership. There seems to be a significant incidence of newspapers being read at the office rather than at home, which is a possible explanation for the perceived drop on Fridays.

There are a number of published magazines. The English-language magazines cater to select niche markets – for example, *Adventure Oman*, *Oman Visitor* and *Oman Today* tend to focus on the Western expatriate community in Oman and cover adventure, entertainment, the outdoors, and so forth. *Oman Economic Review* and *Business Today* are business magazines. *Automan* is a glossy car magazine. The two English dailies also bring out magazines on specific days circulated free with the newspaper. *Thursday*, *ET* (Entertainment Times) and *Money Works* are some examples. Two special magazines brought out on the country's National Day on 18 November are *Tribute* and *Pride*, in honour of Sultan Qaboos bin Said. These magazines are glossy, with well-researched and presented varied facets of Oman as a country. Tradition, culture, heritage, history, development and environment all combine to make this proud nation a jewel of the Middle East.

There is an equal variety of Arabic magazines, but their focus is more of general interest and oriented towards women. *Al Nahda*, *Al Emra'a* and *Al Omaniya* are examples.

Overall, the press in Oman enjoys a fair degree of freedom with often incisive, analytical, and sometimes critical articles on industry. World news in politics, sport and entertainment comes from established international news agencies without apparent or unreasonable censorship. Moral restraint, the absence of sensationalism, non-interference and tolerance amply reflect the values of the nation.

In addition, there is a plethora of directories. The OmanTel Telephone Directory, Yellow Pages, Oman Chamber of Commerce Directory, Business Directory and Guide to Industries all also offer CD ROM listings to advertisers.

Television

Television made a relatively late entry into Oman. Oman TV, the single state-run channel, has played an important role in supporting and protecting local industry through preferential advertising rates and other attractive incentives. Easy access to the gamut of satellite channels has rendered it unnecessary to invest in any more local private channels. Popular programmes on Oman TV include the Arabic news, Arabic serials, sport (particularly football), and occasional films. However, competition from Arabsat channels such as MBC, LBC and Al Jazeera is quite intense and matching the programming quality of these channels is no easy task. Revenues from advertising, so crucial to the development of the medium, have been limited because of the tariff not being cost effective for multinational brands, which are the real big spenders. Local companies, on the other hand, while enthusiastic about the medium, are inhibited by the high production costs of television commercials, as a majority still need to be produced outside the country. Oman TV does, however, offer as an option static caption slides which are more cost effective for smaller domestic clients.

Radio

Oman has two radio channels, which are both state-run: English FM and Arabic FM. Only English FM is open to advertising and broadcasts a reasonable variety of classic and popular music programmes, talk shows, news bulletins and so forth. In spite of an extremely reasonable tariff, use of this medium by advertisers is limited to offers linked with quiz questions on shows. A Sunday evening roadshow has, however, captured the imagination of a wide cross-section, judging by the active participation in phone-ins from across the country. Another audio medium gaining ground is the local 'Talking Pages'. This is a frequently used service in Oman and offers opportunities for advertising messages to be played while customers are placed on hold.

Outdoor advertising

One of the first things that a visitor to Oman notices is its pristine beauty in the form of stark mountains and stunning coastline. Thankfully, skyscrapers and screaming billboards do not mar the skyline. A few neons and strategically placed tri-ads, back-lit posters on pavements along the highway and airport, and bus shelter panels are the limited outdoor advertising options available to advertisers. Naturally, in-shop advertising in supermarkets, malls and showrooms through posters, leaflets, trolley boards and other promotional material is very popular. The high quality of print and production facilities in Oman is apparent from the quality of these materials.

Internet

As with everywhere else in the world, the Internet has grown at a frenetic pace with data on the number of connections becoming dated even before it is collated! However, its spread as an advertising medium has been slow. In the initial flurry, a number of advertisers rushed to take advantage of this new medium through creation of websites. Sadly, the power of the medium was not adequately exploited, with most being content to place their brochures on the web instead of exploiting the rich language of the medium. Some fierce undercutting and low per-page design rates effectively curbed creative development in this medium. OmanTel is currently the only Internet service provider (ISP). There are a few portals such as Sablat Oman, OhiTech and omanaccess. com that take advertising banners, but on the whole this medium is as yet inadequately explored. The use of internationally popular portals such as MSN and Yahoo is more widespread. As local brands expand beyond the borders, and e-commerce becomes a way of life, the power and cost-effectiveness of this live and interactive medium is bound to gain recognition.

Cinema

The crackdown on video piracy in the late 1990s gave a slight shot in the arm to cinema. However, the limited number of halls and seats, the late arrival of Hollywood films and the mainly small audiences (who tend largely to be Asian expatriates) have thwarted commercial use of this medium. Local advertisers find it expensive to produce TV commercials, let alone invest in reverse tele-cine transfers or shooting on 35 mm. Some multinational commercials such as for colas and cars do find their way into cinema halls, as they do not get to air these on Oman TV.

Advertising

Newspapers account for as much as 90 per cent of the total advertising spend in the country. The development of the advertising industry has consequently steered itself towards the development of talent and resources. Leading advertising agencies include OHI DDB, Advertising International Co, United Media Services, Asha and National Publishing and Advertising Co – all full-service agencies. With the singular exception of DDB, the global advertising networks have not established a significant presence in the country.

The total advertising expenditure in the country is estimated at around RO30 million (US$78 million), all inclusive. In the absence of certified data, however, this remains an educated guess. Media planning is largely ad hoc and the final media mix for a brand campaign is driven by judgement and discount considerations rather than any scientific calculations of reach. Cars followed by banks remain the dominant categories in advertising spend (19 out of the top 25 last year were car companies and banks). The gap between these and other categories of advertisers is huge. The advertising also tends to be more skewed towards schemes and promotional offers rather than brand-building thematic advertising. The presence of experienced advertising professionals in the market is, however, apparent in the high standard of creative advertising, particularly in the press and print media.

As an oil-rich country whose entry into the manufacturing arena is relatively new, local 'brands' are few. However, locally manufactured goods are produced to international quality standards and often well above. With the protection provided particularly in the early years to encourage and develop local industry, some of these brands today enjoy a strong monopoly in the country, ahead of international competition. With the slow blurring of commercial borders, it is hoped that these outstanding Omani brands will find their rightful place in international markets through the use of advertising over international media.

7.3

Marketing Research and Public Relations

Suhail Khan, Manager, Marketing Research, SIMPA Marketing Research and Consultancy, Ruwi, and Tausif Malik, Head of Public Relations Division, SIMPA-pr, Ruwi

Introduction

Market research is the function which links the consumer, customer and public to the marketer through information: information used to identify and define marketing opportunities and problems; generate, refine and evaluate marketing actions; monitor marketing performance; and improve understanding of marketing as a process.

Market research

Market research is still in its infancy in Oman but is growing steadily, largely driven by the intensity of focus of a few companies in the country on attaining greater understanding of consumer behaviour.

In the 1980s, the Omani market was a seller's market, the buyers not having much choice. There is a story prevalent in Muscat according to which, during the late 1970s, customers for new pick-up trucks used to congregate at the port waiting for them to be landed and, as soon as the vehicles had come ashore, would throw their turbans into a vehicle, with the owner of the first turban to land in a given vehicle becoming the eventual owner. However, the 1990s witnessed a major change, with a greater assortment of products being available and buyers becoming increasingly knowledgeable and demanding more and more from a product. Thus, the market was transformed into a buyer's market and over time the need for research increased.

SIMPA Marketing Research can be considered the pioneer of market research in Oman. When SIMPA was set up six years ago, there was not a single fully fledged market research agency in Oman. There are a few more foreign research agencies operating in Oman now – such as MEMRB, PARC and AMER, all of which operate throughout the Gulf Cooperation Council (GCC) countries – but their activities are largely restricted to fieldwork in the Sultanate.

SIMPA understands that the success of today's organizations depends on a deep and accurate understanding of customers; thus, the information provided is about what customers think and how they feel, and most importantly, offers insights that help explain why they think and feel in any given way. The questions asked are designed to bring about revealing responses, which are listened to very carefully. Being a local Omani agency, SIMPA has a deeper understanding of the local market as well as of the nuances of Omani society, which has a cultural and behavioural pattern quite distinct from other Arab nations.

As to the other agencies, MEMRB and AMER have both set up retail audit panels in Oman and their strength lies in these areas, and syndicated retail audit information is available with them for about 25–30 product categories. PARC's traditional strength has lain in media research and this remains the case in Oman. For industrial research, consulting companies such as KPMG, PriceWaterhouse Coopers and Ernst & Young also conduct market research studies on behalf of their clients in relation to their projects, usually on a turnkey basis. Along with SIMPA there are a few other economic consultancies – such as Al Baraka Economic Consulting, Future Management and Economic Consultants, Oman House for Economic Consultancy and Tamimah Consultancy Group – which provide clients with demand potential and feasibility study reports on an ad hoc basis.

Research is widely accepted in Oman by the courteous and friendly Omani population. They are usually more than happy to be involved in a research process and only rarely refuse to participate. The main reason for the low refusal rate is perceived to be the use of local field interviewers by SIMPA, who understand local sensitivities and address them accordingly.

Types of research

Market research in Oman can be classified into four broad categories: consumer research, advertising research, business-to-business (B2B) research and industrial research.

In consumer research, the following areas are popular in Oman:

- concept testing and new product development;
- brand and company image and equity research;

- purchase habits and purchase determinants studies;
- consumer product usage and attitudes studies;
- customer satisfaction studies.

In advertisement research, the following types of research are usually conducted:

- copy pre- and post-tests;
- advertisement comprehension studies;
- recall measurement studies.

B2B research is largely need-driven, while industrial research is largely focused on demand potential and feasibility studies.

Plan ahead: long-term versus short-term

The population of Oman is not very large[1] and, as a result, the market for a researcher is sufficiently small in terms of people that its consumer patterns and behaviour can be measured fairly accurately using the appropriate research tools. Even so, business managers continue to shy away from carrying out research and understanding their customers, preferring short-term promotions to gain immediate sales, or to maintain market shares, over long-term achievements likely to be attained if they had a better knowledge of their customers.

The failure of many businesses in Oman can be attributed to the shortsightedness of business managers and a lack of planning. Between 50 per cent and 60 per cent of annual advertising spend in Oman goes into promotion-related activities, with only 25 per cent being spent on brand- or image-building activities. Companies that have a long-term vision and invest in brand building tend to survive longer and be healthier than companies that vie for a share of the pie in the short term. The reasons for the prevalence of this short-term thinking are many, but can be: the result of the local economy being trading oriented; a lack of proper vision; dependency on an expatriate workforce which has to demonstrate immediate results for survival; lack of knowledge of media reach and effectiveness; and the relatively easy entry and exit options which are available to businesses.

Know the market, understand the consumer

An interesting fact that many marketers miss is the population graph: more than 50 per cent of Omanis are under 18 years of age. Allied to this is the government's stress on education, which has ensured that

---

[1] In July 2001, it was estimated at 2,622,198.

the younger generation is better educated with greater knowledge and higher aspirations than their forebears. The advent of women in the workplace is also a recent development which the marketer cannot ignore, as is the double-income young nuclear family electing to set up smaller homes, particularly in urban areas, thereby breaking away from the norms of the past and the large, extended family system, under which several generations lived together under a single roof. Such changes cannot be ignored by the marketer, but frequently are.

Many brilliant marketing ideas which have worked in other Arab countries have fallen flat in Oman because the marketers have ignored the distinctiveness of the Omani market when compared to other GCC or Arab markets. The Omanis are very friendly as well as courteous, while being religious and conservative, but nevertheless are easily accessible and approachable both socially and in business.

With increased competition and the increased aspirations of consumers, as well as the rise in size and knowledge of the younger generations, marketers have increasingly to turn to research in order to understand their target customers. The time has come for companies to segment the market, identify their target customers and position their products so that customers begin to identify with the company and its products. A strongly competitive advantage can be attained in this market by companies that understand and analyse their customers rather than continuing to operate simply by 'gut feel'.

Conclusion

To summarize, while research is emerging as an important tool in Oman as a means of understanding consumer insights and behaviour, it remains in its infancy. It may well take a few years to establish itself as a key strategic decision-making tool, but will nevertheless prove itself in the longer term.

Public relations

Public relations is a virtually non-existent marketing and communication tool in the Omani market. Companies and the media both misunderstand public relations, considering it no more than the issuing and publishing of press releases. There really is very little perception of the needs of a company to raise its profile: for example, with government in regard to policies; with society in regard to corporate responsibilities towards populations and the environment; with employees for the smooth running of operations; with the competition to keep them at bay; with suppliers for regular supply and competitive prices; and with shareholders in regard to the shareholder value and confidence in the underlying business in which they have invested.

The Omani market is a young market compared to others in the Arab world, and thus the evolution of the use of mature marketing tools has been slow but is now gradually taking place. There is, however, a need for the market to be educated about the role of public relations and how it can help in developing and sustaining a brand image.

Public relations is perceived as being very important for Oman at this time, as it has embarked on a programme of privatization, reforms and export-driven market policies which are critical for the country's future success but which nevertheless need to be properly communicated locally and internationally.

Currently, there is a shortage of public relations agencies, interrelated talent and professionalism in the Omani market. However, in 2001, a number of local companies are known to have recruited in-house public relations managers to manage their activities in this field, which is a first sign of corporate comprehension of the need for good communications and public relations. A first step it may only be, but further advances in the sector are expected in the not too distant future.

Part 8

Labour Issues

8.1

Oman Labour Law: Ripe for Reform?

*Majid Al Toky and Juliet Bawtree, Trowers &
Hamlins, Muscat*

Since the promulgation of the Oman Labour Law ('the Labour Law') by
Royal Decree 34/1973 nearly 30 years ago, business organization and
practices in the Sultanate of Oman have developed apace. While a
plethora of ministerial decisions have been issued by the Minister of
labour, some are of the view that the current law does not meet the
requirements of the social and economic developments experienced in
recent times. The Labour Law is currently under government review
in consultation with the State Council and also businesses in Oman.
The new Labour Law is eagerly awaited by businesses, the judiciary
and lawyers alike.

This chapter focuses on the main provisions of the Labour Law, which
must be examined by employers intending to do business and employ a
workforce in Oman. It is not intended as a comprehensive guide to the
many wide-ranging provisions constituting the Labour Law, but does
seek to highlight those areas of the law that are ripe for reform.

Labour Law jurisdiction

The Labour Law applies to Omani and expatriate employees working
in the private sector, and addresses issues such as wages, overtime pay,
leave, working hours, industrial safety, labour disputes, vocational
training and the requirements for the employment of foreign nationals.
It does not apply to government employees such as civil servants, police
and army personnel.

Any condition of employment that infringes the provisions of the
Labour Law is null and void, unless the condition is of greater benefit
to the employee.

Employment of foreign nationals

Labour clearance

Non-Omanis are not permitted to work in Oman unless clearance has been obtained from the Ministry of Manpower, previously called Ministry of Social Affairs, Labour and Vocational Training

Employers hiring foreign employees must complete the relevant application form issued by the Department of Labour and pay the relevant fees. There are certain categories of positions where labour clearance will not be issued because these must be filled by Omanis.

Labour cards

Once Labour clearance has been granted, the employer will apply for a labour card entitling the worker to work in Oman. Labour cards are usually valid for two years. Any delay in issuing or renewing a labour card will result in a fine of RO5 for each month of delay. Foreign employees must undergo a medical test before a labour card can be issued or renewed.

Working visa

Non-Omanis working in Oman must possess a working visa. It is not permitted for a foreigner who entered Oman on a visitor or business visa to engage in any kind of paid job in Oman. A working visa is usually issued for two years, but its expiry date does not necessarily coincide with that of the labour card. A foreign employee holding a working visa is allowed to bring his family to live with him in Oman.

Penalties

There are certain penalties associated with any breach of the provisions of the Labour Law. Such penalties range from fines, repatriation of the employee, and the banning of the employer from obtaining labour clearance for a period of one year.

Employers should be particularly aware of Article 105(b) of the Labour Law, which prohibits an employer from deliberately allowing any of his expatriate workers to serve with another employer. Breaching this provision could result in the employer's imprisonment for up to one month and/or punishment with a fine according to the number of workers found in breach of the law. Therefore, a person who enters into a contract with another person for the supply of labour should be careful to ensure that an employment relationship is not created with the workers supplied by the other party. For example, a direct payment to the workers in question may be interpreted as an action that creates an employment relationship. Recent announcements in the newspapers and inspections carried out on employers show that the labour authorities are taking this matter very seriously. This is because, as a matter of principle, a foreign worker is confined to work for the employer who sponsored him to work in Oman, unless a release letter is obtained allowing him to work for another employer.

Omanization

The concept of Omanization, which is to ensure that the local population is employed to the greatest extent possible, has gathered increasing momentum and importance. Omanization and the creation of opportunities for Omanis to work in the private sector is a fundamental political, social and economic policy of the Omani government. Foreigners intending to do business in Oman are advised to take note of Omanization requirements to avoid any obstacles in conducting their activities. Guidelines issued by the Ministry of Manpower require private companies operating in specified sectors to employ Omani nationals as a certain percentage of their labour force. The percentages range, for example, from 15 per cent in the contracting sector to 60 per cent in the transportation, storage and communication sector.

It should be noted that non-Omanis may not be employed in unskilled or low-skilled work unless there are too few Omanis available to perform such work. In particular, Ministerial Decision 5/1978 states that the following types of work may not be performed by non-Omani workers:

- non-technical work;
- assistant to a technical worker;
- guard or watchman;
- light vehicle driver;
- Arabic-language typist.

Article 3 of Ministerial Decision 127/1994 provides that: 'A cash fine is to be imposed on companies and establishments failing to achieve the required Omanization percentages within the given period. Fines are equal to 50 per cent of the average of the total salaries of expatriate employees, representing a difference between the required Omani percentages and the percentages the establishments have actually achieved.'

Termination of employment contracts

Problematic employment issues can arise from the termination of employment contracts. While the Labour Law has a number of provisions dealing with the termination of employment contracts, some of these are open to interpretation, causing ambiguity. Adhering to the notice period specified in the law or in the contract of employment is not usually a deciding factor in determining whether or not the termination was justified. If the contract is of fixed duration and the employer terminates it prior to its full term, he will be required by the court to provide valid justification in this regard. For offences that are not regarded as dismissible under Article 42 of the Labour Law, three warnings are required in order to terminate an employment contract.

Through Article 42, an employer has the right to dismiss a worker without notice and without recompense for the following reasons:

- if the worker assumes a false nationality or resorts to forgery to obtain work;

- if a worker is absent for more than 10 days in any one year without lawful excuse or more than seven consecutive days, provided that, in the first instance, the employer has given the worker written warning prior to his dismissal when he has been absent for five days;

- if a worker is sent to prison for a year or more for committing a crime or if he has committed a misdemeanour at his place of work, or while carrying out his work, and final judgement has been made against him;

- if the worker commits an offence from which the employer suffers heavy losses, on condition that the employer informs the Ministry of Manpower of the incident within three days of it being substantiated;

- if the worker assaults or abuses his employer or colleagues at his place of work;

- if the worker divulges secrets belonging to the place in which he works;

- if the worker does not abide by instructions for the safety of workers and the work site, in spite of being given a written warning, on condition that such instructions are in writing and are conspicuously displayed.

Some employees have tried to argue that the above are the only reasons for which an employer may fairly terminate a contract. However, the court has confirmed that the list contained in Article 42 is not exhaustive and that the employer may be deemed to have fairly dismissed an employee if he could satisfy the court that the offence committed by the employee is sufficiently serious to the extent that the employer cannot continue employing the employee in question.

In order to be effective, disciplinary measures and the circumstances in which they are taken must be lodged with the Department of Labour and posted on a prominent notice board at the place of work. Many larger businesses in Oman illustrate this by way of a penalty chart.

If the worker wants to be reinstated, he must, within one week of the dismissal, submit his complaint before the Labour Office. Complaints relating to other claims do not require to be filed within one week. The Labour Office has a mediatory role and, if it is found that no settlement could be achieved, the matter will be transferred to the court.

If it is proved that the worker has been unjustifiably dismissed, the employee must either be reinstated or receive a fair compensation as determined by the court. In assessing such compensation, the court will look at the position held by the employee, period of service, the possibility of getting another job and any other factors that may influence the level of compensation. In addition, the employee will be entitled to an 'end-of-service' benefit, and all other benefits to which he is entitled, either by law or by virtue of his contract of employment.

The Labour Law does not contain specified guidelines for the calculation by the court of a 'fair compensation', and this, combined with the fact that the Omani legal system is not precedent-based, makes it difficult for employers to make a decision on whether to terminate an employee's contract.

End-of-service benefit

Article 49 of the Labour Law provides that if a contract of employment is terminated, or it expires, the employer must remunerate the worker for his period of service. This is calculated as a sum equal to 15 days at the employee's final basic salary for each of the first three years of employment, plus 30 days per year for each year following the first three. End-of-service benefit is payable only if an employee has served for more than one year with an employer.

Redundancy

The concept of redundancy is not addressed in the Labour Law. As a result, the mere fact that an employer may have more employees than he needs is not in itself a reason justifying the termination of an employee's contract under Omani law. The courts have, however, allowed redundancies on some occasions, and it is anticipated that the new Labour Law will provide more clarity on this issue.

Conclusion

It is expected that the new law will fill the gap that has been created by the social and economic developments in Oman since the promulgation of the existing Labour Law in 1974. It is also expected that the new law will provide employers and employees with more clarity as to their respective rights, and thereby lessen the chances of a protracted conflict in respect of them and cut down the number of cases brought to court.

The Labour Law provisions summarized above constitute only a fraction of the Labour Law, but their importance must not be underestimated. A company doing business in Oman employing expatriates and Omanis must ensure that it has policies in place to prevent it falling foul of the Labour Law. To do so could cripple a company's ability to successfully conduct business in Oman.

8.2

Human Resource Management: The Challenges Ahead

Gordon C Anderson, Managing Director, GC Anderson Consulting, Nicosia, Cyprus

Introduction

Human resource management (HRM) has developed rapidly on a global scale in recent years, and Oman will benefit from the greater contribution that modern HRM can make to organizations.

The political focus on Omanization has rightly put the spotlight on training. The theme of this chapter is that training alone is unlikely to produce all the benefits that can be expected unless accompanied by modern HRM – the argument being that HRM is required to ensure that people in organizations are effectively managed and motivated and are given the opportunities to apply their skills, develop their careers, and realize their potential.

To identify and analyse current HRM issues in Oman and highlight the requirements for the development of HRM in Oman, it is necessary to review the political, economic and social context.

Political, economic and social context

The past 30 years have seen dramatic economic change in the Sultanate of Oman. Oman has developed into an economic force to be reckoned with. Emerging from a simple economy characterized by agriculture and fishing, supported by the wealth of its oil resources, Oman has seen dramatic development, and now possesses a modern and expansive infrastructure including electrical utilities, telephone services, good roads, modern medical facilities, public education and a rapidly developing higher education sector.

Although the economy once depended on infrastructure projects executed by large multinational contractors, Omani companies have become increasingly established and now play a very significant role in the economy.

Development plans and the importance of HRM

The Sixth Five-Year Development Plan (2001–2005) emphasizes two major economic goals:

- economic diversification to reduce Oman's dependence on oil;

- higher education and HR development.

The diversification objective requires the government to direct investment to non-oil- and non-gas-income-generating sectors, including agriculture, fisheries, mining, light industry and services.

As Dr Fuaad Jaffer Sajwani, vice-president, Central Bank of Oman, pointed out in an article entitled 'Education: the Key to Oman's Future',[1] there is now an urgency to develop HRM, as Oman's natural wealth will not last forever. He stated, 'Human capital will be the only resource left to rely upon to continue economic growth, alongside attracting foreign investment.'

His Majesty Sultan Qaboos made an historic address to the Council of Oman in 2001, in which he placed great urgency on the issues of HR development and Omanization.

> 'Nations are built solely by the hands of citizens. Progress and prosperity can only be achieved through learning, experience, training and qualifications.'

> 'The real power of any nation is made up of its human resources. They are the power that achieves development in all walks of life.'

During the present [Sixth] Five-Year Plan (2001–2005) the government aims to create 110,000 job opportunities compared with 78,000 in the previous Plan.

Future potential

Dr Sajwani cites the example of Singapore in identifying the potential for developing the human assets of Oman. Singapore, he suggests,

---

[1] Dr Fuaad Jaffer Sajwani, 'Education: the Key to Oman's Future', *Oman Economic Review*, May/June 2001.

provides an excellent example in developing labour market policies to boost the indigenous workforce. In 1990, the ratio of economically active Omanis in the age group 15–64 was 41 per cent in 1993 compared to almost 65 per cent in Singapore. For women, the ratio was 7 per cent in Oman against 50 per cent in Singapore. In recent years, considerable progress has been made with respect to these statistics in Oman, but the high percentage of the population under 15 years of age (estimated at 52 per cent of the total population of 1.7 million Omanis in 1998) indicates the need for creating more job opportunities in the future.

The private sector has a large foreign workforce, and Omanization is aimed at encouraging, in a planned way, the replacement of foreign workers by nationals.

In setting up, in 2001, a fund named the 'Sanad' (Support) Project for the Employment of National Manpower, His Majesty the Sultan called on the private sector to take the initiative and play a key role in raising the ratio of Omani labour recruitment in private enterprises in comparison with expatriate workers.

Nature of human resource management (HRM)

HRM is concerned with ensuring that organizations obtain and retain people with the right mix of skills, qualifications and experience to undertake the work of the organization. In increasingly competitive conditions, motivation, productivity and commitment become themes of central importance, and require effective HRM. Motivating and retaining key people and gaining their commitment to the organization become critically important in giving organizations the edge in competitive conditions.

Practical tools for successful HRM

Training and development represent one element of HRM. Modern HRM relies on professional skills in other key areas as shown in Figure 8.2.1.

This diagram identifies the four key 'levers' of HRM, indicating that to achieve the effective utilization of human resources, organizations need to ensure that professional skills and modern techniques are applied in the fundamental areas of:

- recruitment and selection;
- performance appraisal;
- rewards;
- training and development.

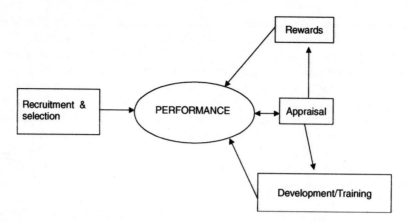

Figure 8.2.1 The Human Resource Management cycle

Figure 8.2.1 demonstrates the need for an integrated approach to HRM – failure in any one area leads to an unsatisfactory situation for the effective use of people.

In addition to focusing on practical policies, HRM is also concerned with:

- supporting the goals and strategies of the business;

- ensuring that leadership styles focus on people issues;

- developing a positive organization culture that emphasizes perform-ance, innovation and commitment.

Present status of HRM

The philosophy and practices of HRM in Oman can be analysed in three main areas:

- *Government sector:* in the government sector, HRM initiatives and policies largely emerge from the Ministry of the Civil Service and are then implemented by other ministries. Saud Al-Yahmadi, Man-ager, Training and Qualifying Department of the Ministry of the Civil Service, explained that this centralized approach has the advantage of ensuring fairness across ministries, and the application of consist-ent standards in, for example, the advertising of vacancies and the selection methods used in filling vacancies. His paper entitled 'Strategic HRD in the Sultanate of Oman',[2] presented at the Human

---

[2] Saud Al-Yahmadi, 'Strategic Human Resource Development in the Sultanate of Oman', paper presented at Human Resources Global Management Conference, Barcelona, 20–22 June 2001.

Resources Global Management Conference in Barcelona in June 2001, showed that HRM has been well developed in the public sector.

- *The large local and international companies in the private sector, primarily related to oil and gas, and to banking.* The companies in this sector, mainly large companies, appear to be the leaders in the development of HRM in Oman. Companies such as Petroleum Development Oman (PDO, a major influence not only in the oil and gas sector but also on many contractors and supplier companies), Shell and Occidental have access to global HR through their international connections. In addition, these companies, as is the case with the major banks, have highly professional Omanis in senior HR roles.

- *The small and medium-sized local companies, often privately owned.* In this sector, the management emphasis has been placed largely on finance – making investment in people seem like a cost. Many companies in this category have yet to introduce modern HRM. In many of the companies that fall into this category, there is still a tendency to equate HRM with personnel administration – processing visas, interpreting the Labour Law, handling leave applications, and so forth. Important though these activities are, they are not HRM.

Evaluation of the present status of HRM

In 'The New Society of Organizations',[3] Peter Drucker stated, 'All organizations now say routinely, "People are our greatest asset." Yet few practise what they preach, let alone truly believe it.'

In Oman, in two of the three areas of organizational activity identified – namely, the public sector and the large private-sector organizations with international connections – HRM is well developed, with the HRM function headed by well-qualified senior managers.

Ghaya Ahmed Al-Riyami, Manager of the Personnel and Human Resources Development Department in a major financial institution, stresses that as the new generation of young Omanis enters the job market, it is imperative to find proper employment for them. She suggests that much has already been achieved in developing strategies that encourage Omanization, and that the transition from expatriates to Omani nationals has been well-handled, particularly with respect to unskilled and semi-skilled workers.

She is of the view that more effort is required in addressing the HR challenges relating to the effective use of professional staff in organizations, in the light of the new economic order characterized by global

---

[3] Peter Drucker, 'The New Society of Organizations', *Harvard Business Review*, Sept/Oct 1992.

competition and the growing importance of 'knowledge' workers in organizations.

Drucker's quotation applies more accurately to the third component of organizational activity – namely the small and medium-sized companies, many of which are family-owned.

One of the factors that may have delayed the development of HRM in small and medium-sized companies has been the absence of professional managers. In the history of the development of the private sector in Oman, many of the big companies were involved in construction, which is a contract-driven business. When contracts are completed, you go home. Thus, there was no time or need to pay attention to HR issues.

Many Omani company owners take a short-term, cost-minimizing approach to the recruitment process. The business philosophy has been to obtain the cheapest possible people to do a job. Competency and qualifications have merely been desired rather than essential prerequisites.

The starting point for change is the need for a paradigm shift – viewing people not as a perishable resource to be administered, but as a valuable commodity to be developed. This requires a significant change of approach, in viewing expenditure on HR and HRM as an enlightened investment rather than an avoidable cost.

Future challenges for HRM

While initiatives placing emphasis on training are highly commendable – and will undoubtedly contribute to the future development of Oman – training alone is not enough, but must be accompanied by the development of HRM in all Omani organizations if the results of the investment in training are to be fully realized.

As long ago as 1988, Tom Peters, in his book *Thriving on Chaos*,[4] was predicting that the successful companies of the future would focus on highly trained, flexible people as the main means of adding value.

Need for increased emphasis on long-term strategic planning and strategic HRM

One of the many challenges in a fast-developing country such as Oman, in which the future emphasis is increasingly being placed upon the private sector, is to encourage companies to change from short-term profit maximization to a longer-term view towards developing strategic goals and plans. A shift towards longer-term strategic planning would also assist the emergence of HRM.

---

[4] Tom Peters, *Thriving on Chaos*, 1988.

HRM strategy can be developed to ensure that the HRM policies are correctly aligned to support the business objectives. This implies that they must be reviewed and modified whenever new business objectives are set. This also implies that a member of senior management should be responsible for HRM, so that HR considerations are taken into account whenever new business strategies are being considered.

Suhail Khan, manager of SIMPA Marketing Research and Consultancy in Muscat, indicated in a recent article[5] that there is at present little strategic thinking in companies. Khan stated, 'Companies need to recognize the importance of planning beyond next year. I do not find companies planning five years ahead.'

Lawrence Alva, a senior expatriate technical training manager, is of the opinion that there is a catching-up process in the whole area of HRM. He states, 'Oman has made incredible progress in its infrastructure, roads, communication systems etc – it now has to ensure that human assets are properly managed and developed. In the past attitudes have focused on the short term; a longer-term planning approach is needed which places emphasis on strategic goals and the development of HRM strategies to support them.'

Language barriers and English language development

Although Arabic is the official language of Oman, English is widely used, particularly in industrial, commercial and financial communications.

Many Omanis, particularly young school leavers, lack a sound command of English, which is increasingly required in private-sector companies. As most of the expatriate workforce at both managerial and non-managerial levels are unable to converse in Arabic, this leads to limited interaction between Omani and expatriate colleagues. In the five years that the author has been in Oman he has observed steadily improving levels of English. Spoken English is not enough, and many able, ambitious Omanis are recognizing the need to develop their written English skills.

Said Al-Hinai, training manager of HSE at the National Training Institute, occupying a management position supervising the work of a large number of senior trainers, states, 'I feel that I need to develop my skills in written English, to progress in my career. I am reasonably confident about my spoken English, but, as is the case with many Omani colleagues, enhanced written English skills will prepare us to be more effective in meeting future business challenges.'

---

[5] Suhail Khan, in Matthew Brockett, 'Mind the Gap', *Oman Economic Review*, January/February 2002.

Organization culture

Robert Kaplin, joint creator of the now world-famous 'Balanced Score-card' concept, writing in a recent article,[6] stated, 'More and more of the work done today is mental. Employees are involved in more discretionary tasks, such as product development, marketing and customer relations. The challenge for organizations today is how to enlist the hearts and minds of all employees.'

Modern HRM tools are required to create performance-enhancing organization cultures. Reward systems are required that recognize, reward and therefore reinforce excellent performance. Challenging goals are agreed and clearly stated to provide direction and a basis for evaluation. The positive values are pervasive throughout the organization, and top management 'lives' the values.

Developing flexible organization cultures characterized by positive values and an emphasis on excellent performance is another area where HRM can make a significant contribution. BankMuscat, for example, has embarked upon an ambitious customer service training programme for all managers and employees, with consulting support from the Education and Training Group of Renaissance Holdings. This should assist in creating a performance-enhancing culture for the largest bank, operating in a highly competitive environment.

Hilal Al-Mawali, HR and Administration Manager for Shell Oman, regards the starting point as a challenge for both individuals and companies to develop realistic attitudes. It is all too easy, he suggests, for young persons to have unrealistic expectations about jobs and job prospects. The situation is gradually improving, but it will take time and represents an educational challenge for both individuals and companies. The desired goal is a situation where companies give emphasis to HRM issues including designing interesting jobs and creating career development opportunities, and where individuals develop positive attitudes towards work and commitment to their employing organizations.

His Majesty Sultan Qaboos has drawn attention to the need for social and attitude change. He has stated that families should instil the love of work and the spirit of cooperation, honesty and self-help in their younger members, and schools should foster creativity and innovation among students.

The government is exerting efforts to create a culture that will help modernize society and correct the negative social attitude towards certain types of jobs.

---

[6] Robert Kaplin, 'Marked Impact', *People Management*, CIPD, London, 25 October 2001.

Role of line managers and HRM specialists

Hilal Al-Mawali sees a number of ways forward for HRM in Oman. He has stated, 'Line managers must possess good initial skills – skills in managing and motivating staff, in setting demanding goals and performance standards, and treating staff fairly and consistently. HRM specialists are advisers in creating appropriate HR policies and procedures and providing advice and support.' The type of approach that he suggests, with HRH a shared responsibility between line managers and HR specialists, is in line with international thinking about how to achieve excellent HR results.

Education for capability

The HRM challenges of effectively managing and motivating professional and 'knowledge' workers have already been identified. Ghaya Ahmed Al-Riyami draws attention to the concept of 'education for capability' or 'fit for purpose'. She states: 'The idea of depending upon passive educational systems is no longer viable when employing individuals, especially graduates, for positions requiring specific skills. Proper training after employment, and constant on-the-job follow-up of how they are undertaking their responsibilities, is required.' She also indicates that addressing HRM issues, and promoting 'education for capability' will be aided by closer cooperation between educational and training institutions.

Conclusion

In addition to the issues identified above, if organizations devote greater attention to the fundamentals illustrated in the HR management cycle – designing and implementing sound systems for recruitment and selection, performance appraisal, rewards, as well as training and development – they will have made considerable progress in shifting the emphasis from traditional personnel management and administration towards the introduction of effective HRM. The results should lead to positive responses by employees and thereby a motivated and productive workforce.

8.3

Training: The Key to Future Development

Renaissance Holdings, Education and Training Group, Madinat Sultan Qaboos

Introduction

Thirty years ago, His Majesty Sultan Qaboos expressed his vision for the renaissance of Oman, emphasizing that to compete in a regional and global economy Oman would have to build its infrastructure on trained and qualified Omani citizens. The Sultan was aware that economic reliance upon the oil reserves of Oman was a future with finite parameters and he assured the Omani people in 1972 that: 'The important thing is that there should be education, even under the shadow of the trees.'

With an infrastructure being built around them, the citizens of Oman were educated in their basic rights: the rights to security, an education and a future. In his speech on National Day in 1980, the Sultan once more declared, 'Steps are to be taken to fit our young people to become the scientists, technicians, doctors, agriculturalists and other specialists whom we shall need in increasing numbers as the process of our modern development continues to gain momentum.'

Just one generation later, this vision of education and training has to a large extent been realized in contributing to Oman's economic self-reliance and diversification. Many challenges lie ahead to ensure the momentum of economic development is sustained, as increasing numbers of young Omanis become available to enter the job market.

Recent developments

Training is one of the main areas of focus in the Sixth Five-Year Development Plan (2001–2005). This emphasis on training is in line with the strategies developed by other nations in placing a central focus on education and training as a key factor in contributing to, and accelerating, balanced economic development. Singapore, for example, provides an excellent illustration of a country that has successfully built a sound economy based on policies concerned with upgrading and supporting high school education, vocational and technical training, as well as higher education. The substantial investment by Singapore in creating a new style of 'knowledge workers' who drive the modern global economy provides a model close to the vision that Oman is actively pursuing.

The increased emphasis on training in Oman is intended to achieve social objectives of reducing unemployment among young Omanis as well as fostering economic growth.

The government has upgraded high school education, and the education system currently turns out approximately 40,000 secondary school students each year. The range of choices available to school leavers, depending on their level of academic achievements, includes, for the highest achievers, Sultan Qaboos University or the University of Sohar, the country's first private university. In addition, there are eight private colleges offering a range of courses, usually to HNC and HND levels, with the possibility of progressing to degree courses.

Each year some of the best students, depending largely on the economic circumstances of their families, pursue higher education overseas, with the United States and United Kingdom being the most likely destinations, although some students continue their studies in a diverse range of countries including India and Malaysia.

In 1993, a Vocational Training Authority (VTA) was established to formulate plans for the training of a national workforce. The objective of this authority was to reduce dependence on expatriate labour and speed up the process of Omanization. As a result of the actions taken by the VTA, the government established the first in a series of industry-specific Omanization quotas and stipulated 'reserved' occupations. In turn, the establishment of quotas gave birth to a number of vocational training institutions. The Omani government has used the NVQ (National Vocational Qualification) system as a means of assessing the competence of students to carry out specific job-related tasks after training.

The government is now placing greater emphasis on the quality of training and as a result instituted a series of quality inspections of all licensed training institutes in October 2001. The United Kingdom's Adult Learning Inspectorate (ALI) carried out the inspections. The inspection programme provides the information needed to set quality standards for all vocational training institutions. The objective of the inspection is to improve quality levels by benchmarking against comparable institutions in the United Kingdom.

Yousuf Al-Rawahi, manager, training, at the Ministry of Manpower, states, 'Trainees have one government-funded opportunity to acquire the vocational skills to ensure job competence, and secure a job at the end of the training period. It is vital that the training they receive is of the highest quality.'

Achievements

A major achievement in training is represented by the successful establishment of the Salalah port, inaugurated on 1 November 1998. Salalah port has been a key development project for the Dhofar region in the south of Oman, providing many new employment opportunities for local people. From the outset in 1998, 61 per cent of the workforce comprised local Omanis trained for their new roles through a coalition of Omani public-sector officials and private-sector professionals from the Netherlands and the United Kingdom.

A collaboration between Salalah Port Services (SPS) and the National Training Institute (NTI), together with its local partners at the Higher Institute for Administrative and Technical Sciences (HIAT) over a two-year period, involved the screening of a total of 1,600 applicants, short-listing 600 for further assessment, before finally selecting 296 on merit for job training.

Most of the trainees had no previous work experience and none had any port-related experience. Since a skilled labour force including many skill groups is essential for the effective operation of the port, this represents a successful illustration of the contribution of training to economic development. In recognition, this project received the award of the Oman Investment Project of the Year in 1999. In 2001, Salalah achieved record-breaking results for container port productivity, an indication of its continuing success.

The future

The new Minister of Manpower has made it clear that he wants to create an atmosphere conducive to partnership between private-sector employers and his ministry in providing high-quality training to young Omanis.

As an example of the kind of new job partnership envisaged, in December 2001 a memorandum of cooperation was signed between the Ministry of Manpower and the Oman Society for Petroleum Services (OPAL – see also Chapter 2.4). This is the first sector-related training initiative. The vision of the partnership is to promote world-class standards of competence and professionalism in the petroleum sector through training policies. The main objective will be to recruit and train

1,000 Omanis for jobs in the oil and gas sector. This will have the impact of changing the present ratio of two expatriates to one Omani, to two Omanis for each expatriate by 2005. The intention is also to implement an apprenticeship programme with accredited examinations and to introduce competence assessment by independent third parties.

This pioneering initiative is likely to be followed by other sector-related partnerships covering other major areas of the economy.

The development of a new IT park in Muscat will also give a boost to investment and employment generation. The first phase of the IT park is planned to open in late 2002.

The number of Omani students leaving schools, colleges and universities will rise substantially to around 60,000 in each of the next five years, creating a significant employment and training challenge for Oman. As Mohammed Al Kharusi, HR director of Petroleum Development Oman (PDO) stated,[7] 'Since most industries in Oman, apart from oil and gas and banking, are in the primary stages of development, human resource development will be critical to government policies. Ideally, a government–corporate partnership should pave the way for a manpower strategic planning unit. Human resource development in Oman would do well to move a step closer to strategic business partnering by understanding the business needs of the future, because results are achieved through people, and it is people that make the difference.'

---

[7] Mohammed Al Kharusi, 'Human Resource Development: a Challenge for the Nation', *Business Today*, January, 2002.

Part 9

The Real Estate Market

Residential and Commercial Property Markets

Michael Lowes, General Manager, Cluttons and Partners, Muscat

Property leasing

Most residential properties and many commercial properties are marketed by agents, who in some cases may also be involved in the management of the property. Agents' boards will often be displayed on properties and websites may be available to give a more comprehensive list of the properties that are available (for an example, visit http://www.cluttons-oman.com).

Agents can arrange viewings of properties and should be in a position to show a range of properties that meet a tenant's requirement. Given the small size of the market and the small geographical area in which expatriates tend to live, it is relatively easy to view a number of properties and become acquainted with the area and the market fairly quickly.

Agents' fees are paid by the landlord on completion of a successful letting and therefore the viewing service is effectively provided free of charge to potential tenants.

Lease agreements

The leasing of property in Oman is covered by a real estate law, which governs the relationship between landlords and tenants, and essentially the same rules apply to both commercial and residential property.

Lease agreements take the standard form of a brief four-page document (two pages in English, two in Arabic) issued by the Municipality. Four copies of the lease are signed by the landlord and tenant, and the lease is then registered with the Municipality after payment of a tax by the landlord. A copy of the stamped lease is then returned to both landlord and tenant and this forms the legal contract agreement between parties.

From the tenant's side, the lease agreement can either be in the name of the company or, in the case of residential property, in the individual occupier's name.

Leases of commercial property will almost exclusively be held in a company name. For such leases, it is necessary for the company to be registered, as a copy of the commercial registration and the authorized signatory registration are required when registering the lease with the Municipality.

Leases of residential property previously tended to be held in a company name, but there has recently been a move by companies to provide a rental allowance to employees, who then take the lease in their individual name. In such cases, a copy of the tenant's passport and labour card are required by the Municipality.

Lease length and termination

The majority of leases, both commercial and residential, cover a period of one year. The lease will be renewed automatically unless either party gives notice not less than three months (or half the lease period if this is less then three months) before the expiry date. There are limited circumstances under which the landlord can request termination of the lease.

Longer leases may be requested by tenants, particularly for commercial properties where expenditure is to be incurred, in order to provide additional security. In such cases, the rent will usually be fixed for the full lease period, which differs from annually renewable leases where the rent could in theory be revised upon renewal.

Rent payment

Rents were traditionally paid annually in advance but more flexible payment terms can now be negotiated with landlords. Typically, three months' rent in advance might now be more common, but landlords are likely to request, particularly when properties are initially leased, that the tenant provides post-dated cheques for the full one-year period.

Residential accommodation

There is a wide range of residential property available for expatriates in Muscat. Accommodation is less expensive than many other Gulf States and, as a result, a high proportion of Western expatriates, particularly those with families, occupy villas rather than apartments.

Villas range very much in quality and price, from RO300 per month up to RO3,000 per month, and are found in a variety of locations. The location will often determine the type of property, with areas having been developed at different times and with some areas being more upmarket than others.

Some villas have been purpose-built for leasing to expatriates while others are private villas where the owner may have decided to lease his property to create an income, often when the property is first built. More recently, some small villa compounds have been constructed and these have the benefit of providing additional facilities, such as swimming pools or sports courts, as well as providing added security.

Apartments also vary very much in quality and price, with properties at the higher end of the market being similarly priced to cheaper villas. A typical good-quality apartment in a modern building should provide adequate accommodation if the block is well maintained, but it is unusual for there to be any additional facilities other than perhaps the provision of a reserved parking space.

The most exclusive apartment building is Hatat House, which has few if any direct competitors in terms of quality and facilities. It provides high-quality apartments with additional facilities, which include underground parking, on-site maintenance, a swimming pool and tennis and squash courts.

The main locations favoured by expatriate tenants are:

Madinat Sultan Qaboos

Madinat Sultan Qaboos was perhaps the original expatriate housing area, with many of the properties having been developed during the 1970s and 1980s specifically for expatriate workers. Accommodation includes individual villas, garden court properties built around a common garden and pool area, and a number of apartment blocks.

These properties are now reasonably dated and in need of refurbishment, with the level of repair and maintenance varying from landlord to landlord. Despite this, however, the area remains relatively popular due to its central location, the neighbourhood shopping centre, which forms part of the development, and the presence of a number of nurseries and the British School.

Qurm

Again, Qurm is an older established residential area that remains popular with expatriates. Properties comprise individual villas of different designs and again the standard of accommodation will reflect the level of maintenance provided as well as the age and quality of the property.

Qurm is located centrally, with the main Muscat to Seeb highway (which passes the international airport out of town) providing easy access to most parts of the capital area. Qurm is bordered to the north by the sea, and many properties – particularly those in elevated positions – enjoy sea views.

Shati Al Qurm

Shati Al Qurm is a more recent development, which runs to the south of the beach between Qurm to the east and Al Khuwayr to the west. The properties comprise mainly good-quality private villas, many of which have been built within the last 10 years.

Shati Al Qurm is regarded as a prestigious residential area with the benefit of the beach and the presence of both the Intercontinental and Grand Hyatt hotels. Again, it is centrally located and is close to the main Muscat to Seeb highway.

Al Khuwayr

Also fairly centrally located, Al Khuwayr contains a mixture of accommodation dating from different periods of development.

The older part of Al Khuwayr is characterized by private residential villas which are generally of a moderate standard and which due to their location and quality are less attractive to expatriate tenants.

The most recent development is Al Khuwayr 33, which has been extensively developed within the last 10 years. Again, it comprises private residential villas which are generally of a moderate standard and which offer relatively good-value accommodation. Previously, this area had no mains water supply, but now most areas have been connected.

Al Khuwayr also contains a large number of apartment blocks, many of which were constructed during the property boom of the early 1990s. While the standard of accommodation varies greatly, the more modern properties generally provide good-quality space.

Ghubbrah

Ghubbrah lies to the east of Al Khuwayr towards the airport and is split by the main highway resulting in the Ghubbrah North and Ghubbrah South designations.

While there are pockets of older properties, Ghubbrah generally contains more modern properties, being mainly private villas of moderate standard. In general, properties in Ghubbrah offer better value for money due to their less central location, although access to Ghubbrah North has improved following completion of a new link road.

Azaiba

Azaiba lies to the east of Ghubbrah North and between the main highway to the south and the coast to the north. It has been almost entirely developed within the last 10 years. As with Ghubbrah, the properties generally comprise private villas of moderate standard.

Access has been much improved by the new road link mentioned above. Again, the properties offer better value for money, which is a reflection of the less central location and the relative lack of other amenities in the area.

Market conditions

The residential lettings market has remained relatively strong over the last few years in comparison to other sectors of the market. This is particularly true with regard to villas in the mid-price range where the number of good-quality properties available has been more or less matched by the continued demand for such properties.

The continued supply of new apartment buildings has seen some softening of rentals but this has affected lower-quality properties to a greater extent. Better-quality properties providing Western-expatriate-standard accommodation have seen some pressure for reduced rental levels, but rents remain fairly stable.

Rental rates

Table 9.1.1 provides figures for a range of properties in each of the above areas. These figures are for guidance only and are based upon modern, good-quality accommodation.

Table 9.1.1 Rental rates

	1-bed apartment (RO per month)	2-bed apartment (RO per month)	3-bed villa (RO per month)	4-bed villa (RO per month)
Madinat Sultan Qaboos	250–350	300–350	400–600	600–900
Qurm	250–350	300–450	500–700	700–1,000
Shati Al Qurm	300–400	400–600	600–800	700–1,000
Al Khuwayr	200–250	300–400	450–600	600–900
Ghubbrah	150–250	250–400	400–500	500–800
Azaiba	150–250	250–400	400–500	500–800

Note: RO1 = GBP1.84 approximately.

Commercial property market

Offices

The traditional office area used to be the Central Business District (CBD), which is located in Ruwi some 30 kilometres to the east of Seeb International Airport. This was traditionally the commercial heart of

Muscat and was developed with a number of mid-rise buildings housing the headquarters and offices of all of the major international and local banks, financial services companies, travel agencies, and the offices of a number of the major local trading companies. Subsequent additions were the Muscat Securities Market (MSM) and the Central Bank of Oman.

In recent years, two major changes have taken place in this area: the relocation of companies to other areas and the development of new office buildings in the CBD South area. Due to the availability of office buildings in other areas, which were either closer to customers and/or closer to residential areas, a number of companies have moved out of the CBD area and no longer regard it as a prime location. Those companies that have remained or that plan to be located in this area are principally those involved in financial services where the location of the bank head offices, the MSM, Central Bank and related organizations is of importance. The amount of space available in the CBD area has increased dramatically in recent years with the development of new properties in the CBD South area located to the rear of the MSM and Ministry of Commerce and Industry. One very large office building has been completed together with a series of smaller buildings and others are currently under construction.

The alternative locations for occupiers outside of the CBD are Qurm, Wutayyah and Al Khuwayr. In these areas, office buildings are not concentrated together as in the CBD, but a range of properties are available.

Qurm and Wutayyah are located close together and lie to the west of the CBD area towards the residential areas of Madinat Sultan Qaboos, Al Khuwayr and Shati Al Qurm. There are a number of office buildings in these areas that also contain commercial activity, with Qurm being the location of a number of shopping centres and Wutayyah being the location of most of the car showrooms. This location is close to the CBD but avoids some of the problems of this area such as traffic congestion and parking shortage. The commercial nature of the area has also helped to attract several tenants who welcome visits from members of the public, including airline offices (British Airways and KLM) and insurance companies (Northern Assurance). The area is also close to Petroleum Development Oman (PDO) and is therefore attractive to companies involved in the oil business.

Al Khuwayr is in fact home to a large amount of office space as it is the location of a number of government ministries which are all grouped together on the northern side of the main Muscat to Seeb highway. These are all government-owned buildings, which are effectively outside the 'office market'. To the rear of the ministry buildings are a large number of Embassies, which again are grouped together in one location close to the beach. The other office buildings in the area are in a variety of locations in Al Khuwayr, with a number of buildings on the main service road, directly to the south of the Muscat to Seeb highway, containing retail space on the ground floor and office space on the upper floors.

In other locations to the west of Al Khuwayr towards the airport, such as Ghubbrah and Azaiba, there is some additional office space. This generally tends to be space that is owner-occupied as head-office premises with little speculative office development. Office space will often be provided in conjunction with manufacturing, warehousing and storage facilities.

Market conditions

The office market is weak at present due to limited demand and an increased supply of available space. This has created a tenants' market with landlords competing for occupiers and willing to offer extremely competitive terms in order to secure deals.

The market in Muscat has always been rather unusual, with large sectors being owner-occupiers such as the many government bodies mentioned above. In addition, there are a number of local family-owned trading houses, which between them control a significant portion of business in Oman. These companies again tend to a large extent to be owner-occupiers, which are, therefore, effectively removed from the office market as potential tenants.

The economy has been slow in recent years, which has meant that there has been no real increase in demand for office space. Very few companies have been expanding and many new lettings have simply been companies relocating from one building to another.

At the same time, there have been new developments coming on stream, which have increased the supply of available space. This has combined with the lack of demand to create the current market conditions. Often, tenants will move to new properties at lower rents than they are paying or can upgrade to a new building from poorer-quality accommodation without increasing their rental commitment.

Rental rates

Current rental rates are below those that existed three or four years ago and attractive deals can now be secured by tenants. As a general indication of the market changes, the standard rate for good space in the CBD area previously was approximately RO4 per square metre per month, whereas space can now be secured for approximately RO3 per square metre per month. In Qurm, Wutayyah and Al Khuwayr, while there is less of an oversupply situation at present, there is a similar situation with the competitive rates that are available.

Typical rates include:

- CBD area   RO3.000 – 3.500 per square metre per month
- Qurm and Wutayyah   RO3.000 – 3.500 per square metre per month
- Al Khuwair   RO3.000 – 3.500 per square metre per month
- Ghubbrah and Azaiba RO2.000 – 2.500 per square metre per month

With regard to the rates stated above, the following should be noted:

- Rates quoted are applicable for reasonable buildings providing good-quality accommodation comparable with other properties in the market.

- Rates are assumed to be for new lettings rather than lease renewals.

- Office space is leased as a shell, with ceiling finish, lighting and air-conditioning units provided.

- All utilities including air-conditioning charges are billed to the tenant.

- The lease is of standard Municipality format for a period of one or two years in line with market practice.

- Rates may vary for small/large space users and depending upon the length of lease and payment terms.

Retail premises

The main focus of retail activity centres on the Qurm area where there are a series of small shopping centres, many of which were constructed during the early 1990s. This situation may be due to change following the completion of Al Futtaim's city centre development and the imminent completion of Ajay Enterprises' Markaz Al Bahja complex, which are both located beyond the airport at Mawaleh. These two schemes at Mawaleh are expected to attract residents living beyond the airport in areas such as Seeb and Al Hail, together with residents of Ghubbrah and Azaiba – but will almost certainly also draw residents of the capital area (Muscat, Muttrah and Ruwi).

Market conditions

The retail market is relatively slow as retailers report moderate levels of trade, which generally reflects the overall economic climate. The main existing shopping areas and centres continue to enjoy relatively high levels of occupancy, with rental rates having been static for some time. At this time, the effect of the two new centres detailed above is unknown, although it is likely that they will have an adverse effect on many existing retailers.

Rental rates

Rental rates for retail units in shopping centres depend upon the size of the unit and the floor upon which the unit is located. As a general rule, the best centres will average around RO7.000–8.000 per square metre per month for their lettable space, although the new city centre development is achieving rents well in excess of these figures due to its size and status. Many mixed-use commercial/residential buildings have showroom space on the ground floor and, depending upon unit size and building location, these are typically let for around RO3.000–5.000 per square metre per month.

Factories and warehousing

Industrial units and warehousing are found in three main areas – namely, Al Wadi Al Kabir, Ghala and the Rusayl Industrial Estate.

Al Wadi Al Kabir is located close to Ruwi and the CBD area, and is approximately 30 kilometres to the east of the airport. This area contains a large number of car repair workshops, other workshops used for light manufacturing, storage warehouses and labour-camp-type facilities.

The Ghala industrial area is located closer to the airport and lies to the south of the main Muscat to Seeb highway. It is a large area, which again contains a wide range of properties including workshops, manufacturing premises, storage warehouses and labour-camps.

The third area is the Rusayl Industrial Estate, which is a government-owned industrial estate, located close to the Nizwa road lying approximately 10 kilometres to the west of the airport, which is, in turn, west of the capital area. This is a relatively large industrial estate, which has been developed in phases and which provides serviced plots and advanced factory units. The plots are fully serviced with estate roads, electricity, water, gas and drainage. There are also government industrial estates at Sohar, Raysut (Salalah) and Nizwa.

Market conditions

For properties such as these, there tends to be little development specifically aimed at the rental market (with the exception of the industrial estates), with most properties being owner-occupied. Properties that do come on to the rental market may well be those that are surplus to the requirements of the owner. As such, it is difficult to comment on the demand/supply situation that exists at the present time, although the fact that rental levels appear to have remained at a constant level would suggest that the market remains stable.

The demand for and availability of land and buildings on the government industrial estates generally depends upon location. Rusayl and

Sohar are well developed, whereas Raysut and Nizwa have greater availability.

Rental rates

In the Ghala area, much of the land is leasehold at a ground rent of RO0.400 per square metre per year and, due to the fact that all the plots are allocated, these leasehold interests have a value – although substantially less than equivalent freehold plots. On the government industrial estates, serviced plots are available on a 25-year lease. The rental rate is RO0.250 per square metre per year for the first five years of the lease and RO0.500 per square metre per year for the remainder of the lease.

The accepted rental rate for good-quality storage/industrial premises is RO1.000 per square metre per month in the capital area, with poorer-quality space being in the region of RO0.750–RO0.500 per square metre per month. On the government industrial estates, rental rates for advance factory units are calculated on a formula based upon land rental and the cost of the building.

Part 10

General Aspects of Business Culture

10.1

Cross-Cultural Considerations for Life and Business in Oman

Jeremy Williams OBE, Handshaikh Ltd, UK and Dubai

Your company has offered you the appointment of resident company representative in Oman. Where do you start to learn about Oman? Start here before you lose yourself in 'fact finding' and miss the main point that it is 'people' and 'relationships' that matter most in Oman.

First, clear your mind of misconceptions of Arab geography and terminology. The western boundary of 'the Middle East' is usually regarded to be that between Libya and Egypt, while 'the Gulf' comprises the six Gulf Cooperation Council (GCC) countries of Kuwait, Saudi Arabia, Bahrain, Qatar, the United Arab Emirates and the Sultanate of Oman. Take care with the expressions 'the Arabian Gulf' and 'the Persian Gulf' since the shoreline is shared between Arabia and Iran (Persia). The inhabitants of Iran are not Arabs, nor Semitic; they are Indo-Europeans whose tongue is Farsi, not Arabic. Arabic, of course, is the language of the Muslim world – which spreads far beyond the bounds of 'the Middle East' or 'the Arab World'. The latter consists generally of three areas: the Northern (or Levantine) region, North Africa, and the Arabian Peninsula and Gulf states. Some commentators find that the categories of rich/poor, old/new and stable/unstable, malevolent/benevolent dictatorships are useful divisions for grouping the countries of the Arab World.

Second, and importantly, do not give much credence to those who, having lived for a number of years in one part of the region, e.g., Kuwait, now offer to advise you on Oman because they 'know all about the Arabs' since 'Arabs are all the same'. They do not have personal experience of the part of the Arab world in which you are now interested (i.e., Oman) and 'part' is the significant word here; nation is not really good enough since there are differences within the Gulf countries themselves. For example, in Oman there are differences between the north and south of the country, and between those in or near the capital Muscat and those outside. Thus, do your homework on your part of the Arab world – your part of Oman – and do not mentally group it with other parts. Learn, for example, the strong tribal and seafaring heritage of Oman and its influence today.

Third, the expression 'the Arabs' is as unhelpful a demographic expression as 'the Europeans'. Some similarity may exist internally within each grouping in terms of political systems or religion for example (e.g., Islam, an essential ingredient within the Arab world), but it is never wise to regard those who form 'the Arabs' (or 'the Europeans') as though they have the same personal characteristics. People are different everywhere. What is normal behaviour for you may be wholly abnormal behaviour elsewhere.

Your company has been sensible and has paid for you and your spouse to spend a week in Oman some months before you are due to take up residence. You have assembled the facts that really matter to a family: schooling; housing; travel; and visas. Things are looking good. You have met someone who says he hopes to be your sponsor (see below), who is charming and knows all about your company and its expectations. Your children are excited at the prospect of living abroad. Your spouse is content. You know what your company expects of you and you have a decent line manager to whom you report at head office. Both of you have worked well together before. You are reasonably content with the allowances and emoluments that will affect you and your family at your new destination. The goods and services that your company offers sell well to the rest of the world and thus the Gulf will be much the same (presumably). You have high standards and high expectations. You now want the job. You are keen. You can apply the same marketing techniques in the Gulf as anywhere else. What could possibly go wrong?

Alas, you have only scratched the surface of the situation. Now address the 'hassle factor', the 'personal' and the 'personnel' elements. Do you have any idea of the way in which Arab nationals actually conduct their business? Does your head office really have the arrogance to believe that its own standards, habits and methods will simply 'read across' to the Gulf? Why would that be? What presumption! Even though Oman – and the other Gulf countries generally – have had considerable exposure to the West (mainly from the United Kingdom previously, but now from the United States), it has its own methods of reaching decisions, and these are methods that may seem wholly illogical to you and your head office, but are nevertheless perfectly effective in Oman.

Focus urgently on your sponsor. Do you understand what 'sponsor' means in Omani terms? Does your company understand that a relationship with a 'sponsor' is effectively a 'Catholic marriage' because severance is not normally possible regardless of the performance of the individuals concerned on either side? The selection of the company sponsor is the single most important act of any company new to Oman (or to the Gulf generally). Who is he? Who knows him? What is his reputation? Who else has offered his services as your company sponsor? Has any relationship between your company and a sponsor been decided? Who in your company has been involved in the process? Do you trust that person's judgement in terms of his or her exposure to Gulf Arabs and the importance of the subject? Has an agreement actually been signed? Be clear and robust on this next point: if there is the slightest doubt in your mind that the process of sponsor selection has been handled casually by your company, and if – fortunately – there is no agreement in place, demand that your company delays closure until the whole subject has been closely examined and approved at board level. If an agreement is already in place, ensure that your line manager at home understands the details of the relationship and the risks involved.

Gulf law, regulations and practice are generally very much on the side of the Gulf national and national company. Outside certain Free Zones, most companies are owned or controlled by Gulf nationals or Gulf companies (although Oman does now allow 70 per cent foreign ownership under defined circumstances); exclusive foreign ownership is as good as unknown, although some opportunities for 99-year leases are being granted in the United Arab Emirates, and Bahrain does permit 100 per cent foreign ownership for specified types of company. Increasingly, young Gulf Arabs (50 per cent of the GCC countries' population is less than 15 years old) are expecting employment by right and their laws demand – for good reason – that all companies take on more nationals. 'Omanization' is a central, firm requirement of the Omani government and this demand must be kept in mind at all times. Many nationals – who form the minority of Gulf populations – are excellent employees (and managers), but many come from a family where great wealth has been the norm for perhaps two generations. The 'work ethic' has therefore not been a prominent Gulf Arab characteristic, nor has 'good timekeeping' – always a favourite cross-cultural subject noted by Westerners whose watches and diaries usually dominate their lifestyle. However, in Oman, such traits are less prominent since the background of most Omanis is not one of vast family wealth; the young Omani has always known that personal effort and contribution will be needed to achieve success. A simple example of the difference between business life in Oman and certain other Gulf countries is that the Westerner will find it possible to book an appointment with an Omani and for the agreed meeting actually to take place when expected. In some other parts of the Gulf, attendance at meetings by Gulf nationals at prior-agreed times and days is by no means guaranteed.

The problems of gaining access to local decision-takers will come to govern your endeavours in the Gulf, although less so in Oman for the reasons given. It will be essential that you have a genuine friend at head office who understands the way of life of the Gulf. You need protection from those back home who believe that you have somehow, in Western terms, 'gone funny' – for example, you cannot even accomplish the simplest of tasks, such as obtaining from the customer a straight answer to a straight question, or obtaining a timely programme for the CEO's Gulf visit. Without such a friend, your stature in head office may well plummet and your promotion prospects may suffer unfairly since your former colleagues have no idea of what you are undergoing, or how to judge it. 'I managed to speak to Shaikh Abdullah in private for five minutes today about our project. I'm very happy. He said he would think about it all' might be a remark you make in innocence on the telephone to head office, but such a remark will only confirm to many there that you really have become 'odd', whereas the remark should have demonstrated that you have managed to gain the most respectable access to a most powerful person. You are not 'odd' at all; you deserve the highest congratulation from the board. To gain access needs good luck and good exposure to, and understanding of, local practice. 'Access' is the key to everything in the Gulf. It takes time and effort to achieve.

Things are different in the Gulf. Things can happen very quickly after perhaps months or years of waiting. Once an important person has focused on a topic, instructions are given that cause actions to occur that can astound Western expatriates by both their speed and their nature. Gulf Arabs are dismayed that others – Westerners – cannot behave with the same flexibility and speed as they can. The solution is to understand the 'culture' of 'your' part of the Gulf (Oman), and to have the grace and personality to adapt to it accordingly.

Material things – housing, hotels, swimming pools etc – are usually more than satisfactory; this is not the main point to bear in mind when considering employment in the Gulf. The mental stresses and strains must be discovered since it is these that can ruin careers and break marriages. Thus, do your homework on more than just the 'facts' of Oman; look behind these to the more important cross-cultural factors and decide if you have the character (and company back-up and funding) to stay the pace. Pack patience and resilience in your hold baggage and happily pay the excess baggage charge for these two essential Gulf items.

Memo to all HR departments: Do not send impatient people to the Gulf. If there is no choice, then start the re-selection process again, ready for about a year's time. This is about when the current – impatient – incumbent will blow up and have to be replaced.

Finally, 11 September 2001. The long-term effects of the tragedies in the United States in terms of their international impact are, with one exception, unclear. In terms of preparing, as a Westerner, for life or business in the Gulf, the exception is the overwhelming need to study the facts of Islam. Westerners are usually ignorant – perhaps fearful – of Islam and this lack of Western knowledge of a great religion has become dangerous and open to abuse.

Appendices

Appendix I

Useful Addresses

(NB. Both six- and seven-figure telephone numbers are in use)

Chamber of Commerce and Industry

Oman Chamber of Commerce and Industry (OCCI)
PO Box 1400
Ruwi, PC 112
Sultanate of Oman
Tel: (+968) 707684, 707674
Fax: (+968) 708497
E-mail: pubrel@omanchamber.org
Website: http://www.omanchamber.org

Ministries and Business-related Government Agencies

Ministry of Commerce and Industry
PO Box 550
Muscat, PC 113
Sultanate of Oman
Tel: (+968) 771 3500
Fax: (+968) 771 7239
Website: http://www.mocioman.com

Ministry of Oil and Gas
PO Box 551
Muscat, PC 113
Sultanate of Oman
Tel: (+968) 603333
Fax: (+968) 696972

Ministry of Finance

PO Box 506
Muscat, PC 113
Sultanate of Oman
Tel: (+968) 738201
Fax: (+968) 740654

Central Bank of Oman

PO Box 1161
Ruwi, PC 112
Sultanate of Oman
Tel: (+968) 702222
Fax: (+968) 702253
E-mail: markazi@omantel.net.om
Website: http://www.cbo/oman.org

Tender Board

PO Box 787
Al Khuwayr, PC 133
Sultanate of Oman
Tel: (+968) 602583

Public Establishment for Industrial Estates (PEIE)

PO Box 2
Rusayl, PC 124
Sultanate of Oman
Tel: (+968) 626080
Fax: (+968) 626053
E-mail: info@peie.com, rusayl@omantel.net.om
Website: http://www.peie.com

Oman Development Bank SAOG

PO Box 3077
Ruwi, PC 112
Sultanate of Oman
Tel: (+968) 771 2507 / 8
Fax: (+968) 771 3100
E-mail: odebe@omantel.net.om
Website: www.odboman.com

Omani Centre for Investment Promotion and Export Development (OCIPED)
PO Box 25
Al Wadi Al Kabir, PC 117
Sultanate of Oman
Tel: (+968) 771 2344
Fax: (+968) 771 0890
E-mail: info@ociped.com
Website: http://www.ociped.com

Export Credit Guarantee Agency (ECGA)
PO Box 3077
Ruwi, PC 112
Sultanate of Oman
Tel: (+968) 771 3979, 771 3980
Fax: (+968) 771 2380
E-mail: info@ecgaoman.com
Website: http://www.ecgaoman.com

Muscat Securities Market (MSM)
PO Box 3265
Ruwi, PC 112
Sultanate of Oman
Tel: (+968) 771 2607, 771 2621
Fax: (+968) 771 6353, 771 2691
Website: http://www.msm.gov.om

Sultanate of Oman Capital Market Authority
PO Box 3359
Ruwi, PC 112
Sultanate of Oman
Tel: (+968) 771 2607
Fax: (+968) 771 7461
Website: http://www.msm.gov.om

Petroleum Development Oman (PDO)
PO Box 81
Muscat, PC 113
Sultanate of Oman
Tel: (+968) 675370
Fax: (+968) 675654
Website: http://www.pdo.co.om

Embassies

Austria
PO Box 2070
Ruwi, PC 112
Sultanate of Oman
Tel: (+968) 793135, 793145
Fax: (+968) 793669

Belgium
PO Box 808
Muscat, PC 113
Sultanate of Oman
Tel: (+968) 563011, 562033
Fax: (+968) 564905

Denmark
PO Box 1040
Ruwi, PC 112
Sultanate of Oman
Tel: (+968) 703289, 708304
Fax: (+968) 793892

France
PO Box 208
Madinat Sultan Qaboos, PC 115
Sultanate of Oman
Tel: (+968) 681800
Fax: (+968) 681843

Germany
PO Box 128
Ruwi, PC 112
Sultanate of Oman
Tel: (+968) 773 2482, 773 2164
Fax: (+968) 773 5690

Italy
PO Box 3727
Ruwi, PC 112
Sultanate of Oman
Tel: (+968) 564838, 560968
Fax: (+968) 564846

Japan
PO Box 3511
Ruwi, PC 112
Sultanate of Oman
Tel: (+968) 601028, 603464, 600095
Fax: (+968) 698720

Netherlands
PO Box 3302
Ruwi, PC 112
Sultanate of Oman
Tel: (+968) 603706
Fax: (+968) 603397

United Kingdom
PO Box 300
Muscat, PC 113
Sultanate of Oman
Tel: (+968) 693077, 693086 (Commercial Section)
Fax: (+968) 693087

United States
PO Box 202
Madinat Sultan Qaboos, PC 115
Sultanate of Oman
Tel: (+968) 698989, 699049 (Commercial Department)
Fax: (+968) 699778

Airport

Seeb International Airport
PO Box 58
Seeb, PC 111
Sultanate of Oman
Tel: (+968) 519809 (Airport Information)
(+968) 519223, 519456, 519173 (Flight Information)

Hotels

AlBustan Palace
Tel: (+968) 799666
Fax: (+968) 799600
E-mail: albustan@interconti.com

Crowne Plaza
Tel: (+968) 560100
Fax: (+968) 560650
E-mail: mcthc@interconti.com

Grand Hyatt Muscat
Tel: (+968) 641234
Fax: (+968) 605282
E-mail: hyattmct@omantel.net

Muscat Holiday Inn
Tel: (+968) 687123
Fax: (+968) 680986
E-mail: mcthinn@omantel.net.om

Hotel Intercontinental Muscat
Tel: (+968) 600500
Fax: (+968) 600012
E-mail: muscat@interconti.com

Radisson SAS Hotel Muscat
Tel: (+968) 687777
Fax: (+968) 687778
E-mail: muscat.reservations@radissonsas.com
muscat.sales@radissonsas.com

Sheraton Oman
Tel: (+968) 799899
Fax: (+968) 795791, 789513
E-mail: sheraton@omantel.net.om

Sheraton Qurum Resort
Tel: (+968) 605945
Fax: (+968) 605968
E-mail: sheraton@omantel.net.om

Salalah Holiday Inn
Tel: (+968) 235333
Fax: (+968) 235137
E-mail: hinns@omantel.net.om

Hilton Salalah
Tel: (+968) 211234
Fax: (+968) 210084
E-mail: sllbc@omantel.net.om
Website: http://www.hilton.com

Hotel Mercure AlFalaj
Tel: (+968) 702311
Fax: (+968) 795853
E-mail: accorsales@omanhotels.com
Website: http://www.omanhotels.com

Car Hire (Seeb International Airport)

Avis Rent-a-Car
Tel: (+968) 519176
E-mail: avisoman@omantel.net.om

Budget Rent A Car
Tel: (+968) 510816
E-mail: budgetom@omantel.net.om

Europcar
Tel: (+968) 519014
E-mail: eurmct@omantel.net.om

Hertz Rent-A-Car
Tel: (+968) 521187
E-mail: nttoman@omantel.net.om

Business Services

Audit and Accountancy Services

Ernst & Young
PO Box 1750
Ruwi, PC 112
Sultanate of Oman
Tel: (+968) 703105
Fax: (+968) 702734
Website: http://www.eyme.com

Arthur Andersen & Co
PO Box 3482
Ruwi, PC 112
Sultanate of Oman
Tel: (+968) 796983, 797810
Fax: (+968) 797403
E-mail: andersa@omantel.net.om

KPMG
PO Box 641
Ruwi, PC 112
Sultanate of Oman
Tel: (+968) 709181
Fax: (+968) 700839
E-mail: kpmgoman@omantel.net.om

PricewaterhouseCoopers
PO Box 3075
Ruwi, PC 112
Sultanate of Oman
Tel: (+968) 563717
Fax: (+968) 564408
E-mail: oman.pwc@om.pwcglobal.com

Legal Consultants

Trowers & Hamlins
PO Box 2991
Ruwi, PC 112
Sultanate of Oman
Tel: (+968) 771 5500
Fax: (+968) 771 5544
E-mail: trowers@omantel.net.om

Denton Wilde Sapte
PO Box 3552
Ruwi, PC 112
Sultanate of Oman
Tel: (+968) 564346
Fax: (+968) 564395
E-mail: dws@dwsmuscat.com

Intellectual Property/TMP Agents

Abu-Ghazaleh Intellectual Property
TMP Agents
PO Box 2366
Ruwi, PC 112
Sultanate of Oman
Tel: (+968) 560740
Fax: (+968) 563249
Website: http://www.agip.com

Management Consultancy (Marketing: Business-to-Business)

ASA Consulting
PO Box 238
The Ridings
Cobham
Surrey KT11 2WP
United Kingdom
Tel: (+44) 1372 844317
Fax: (+44) 1372 844437
E-mail: asaconsult@btinternet.com

Management Consultancy (Business Development & Marketing: Business-to-Business)

Philip Dew Consultancy Limited
PO Box 11836
Bahrain
Tel: (+973) 790886
Fax: (+973) 790729
E-mail: pdew@batelco.com.bh

Chartered Surveyors/Property Consultants

Cluttons & Partners LLC
PO Box 1475
Ruwi, PC 112
Sultanate of Oman
Tel: (+968) 564250, 564251
Fax: (+968) 564257
E-mail: cluttons@omantel.net.om

Market Research and Public Relations

SIMPA Marketing Research & Consultancy
PO Box 208
AlHarthy Complex, PC 118
Sultanate of Oman
Tel: (+968) 701930, 701430
Fax: (+968) 701242
E-mail: simpa@omantel.net.om

Insurance Services

Norwich Union Insurance (Gulf) Limited
PO Box 833
Ruwi, PC 112
Sultanate of Oman
Tel: (+968) 694040
Fax: (+968) 692739
E-mail: nuigoman@omantel.net.om

Advertising Services

Advertising & Publicity Co (OHI/DDB)
PO Box 889
Muscat, PC 113
Sultanate of Oman
Tel: (+968) 600789, 607415
Fax: (+968) 602746
E-mail: radha@ohigroup.com

Business Publications

Oman Economic Review
United Media Services
PO Box 3305
Ruwi, PC 112
Sultanate of Oman
Tel: (+968) 700895/6
Fax: (+968) 780025
Website: http://www.OERonline.com

Business Today
Apex Publishing
PO Box 2616
Ruwi, PC 112
Sultanate of Oman
Tel: (+968) 799388
Fax: (+968) 793316
Website: http://www.apexstuff.com

Exhibitions and Conferences

Events International
PO Box 268
Ruwi, PC 112
Sultanate of Oman
Tel: (+968) 561073, 561086
Fax: (+968) 561176
E-mail: events@omantel.net.om

Training Services

National Training Institute
PO Box 267
Madinat Sultan Qaboos, PC 115
Sultanate of Oman
Tel: (+968) 605273
Fax: (+968) 605970, 607720
Website: http://www.tawoos.com/nti

Appendix II

Contributors' Addresses

(NB. Both six- and seven-figure telephone numbers are in use)

Abu-Ghazaleh Intellectual Property
TMP Agents
PO Box 2366
Ruwi, PC 112
Sultanate of Oman
Tel: (+968) 560740
Fax: (+968) 563249
Website: http://www.agip.com

Advertising & Publicity Co (OHI/DDB)
PO Box 889
Muscat, PC 113
Sultanate of Oman
Tel: (+968) 600789, 607415
Fax: (+968) 602746
E-mail: radha@ohigroup.com

ASA Consulting
PO Box 238
The Ridings
Cobham
Surrey KT11 2WP
United Kingdom
Tel: (+44) 1372 844317
Fax: (+44) 1372 844437
E-mail: asaconsult@btinternet.com

Cluttons & Partners
PO Box 1475
Ruwi, PC 112
Sultanate of Oman
Tel: (+968) 564250, 564251
Fax: (+968) 564257
E-mail: cluttons@omantel.net.om

Ernst & Young
PO Box 1750
Ruwi, PC 112
Sultanate of Oman
Tel: (+968) 703105
Fax: (+968) 702734
Website: http://www.eyme.com

Export Credit Guarantee Agency (ECGA)
PO Box 3077,
Ruwi, PC 112
Sultanate of Oman
Tel: (+968) 771 3979, 771 3980
Fax: (+968) 771 2380
E-mail: info@ecgaoman.com
Website: http://www.ecgaoman.com

GC Anderson Consulting (Cyprus)
c/o Renaissance Holdings
Education & Training Group
PO Box 267
Madinat Sultan Qaboos, PC 115
Sultanate of Oman
Tel: (+968) 605273
Fax: (+968) 607720
Website: http://www.tawoos.com/nti

Handshaikh Ltd
PO Box 123
Alresford
Hampshire SO24 0ZF
United Kingdom
Tel: (+44) 1962 771699
Fax: (+44) 1962 771814
Tel: (+971 4) 351 7624 (Dubai)
Fax: (+971 4) 352 1033 (Dubai)
E-mail: mail@handshaikh.com
Website: http://www.handshaikh.com

Ministry of Commerce and Industry
PO Box 550
Muscat, PC113
Sultanate of Oman
Tel: (+968) 771 3500
Fax: (+968) 771 7239
Website: http://www.mocioman.com

Muscat Securities Market (MSM)
PO Box 3265
Ruwi, PC 112
Sultanate of Oman
Tel: (+968) 771 2607, 771 2621
Fax: (+968) 771 6353, 771 2691
Website: http://www.msm.gov.om

Norwich Union Insurance (Gulf) Limited
PO Box 833
Safeway Building
Al Khuwayr
Ruwi, PC 112
Sultanate of Oman
Tel: (+968) 694040
Fax: (+968) 692739
E-mail: nuigoman@omantel.net.om

Oman Development Bank (ODB)
PO Box 3077
Ruwi, PC 112
Sultanate of Oman
Tel: (+968) 771 2507 / 8
Fax: (+968) 771 3100
E-mail: odebe@omantel.net.om
Website: http://www.odboman.com

Omani Centre for Investment Promotion and Export Development (OCIPED)
PO Box 25
Al Wadi Al Kabir, PC 117
Sultanate of Oman
Tel: (+968) 771 2344
Fax: (+968) 771 0890
E-mail: info@ociped.com
Website: http://www.ociped.com

Philip Dew Consultancy Limited
PO Box 11836
Bahrain
Tel: (+973) 790886
Fax: (+973) 790729
E-mail: pdew@batelco.com.bh

Renaissance Holdings
Education & Training Group
PO Box 267
Madinat Sultan Qaboos, PC 115
Sultanate of Oman
Tel: (+968) 605273
Fax: (+968) 607720
Website: http://www.tawoos.com/nti

Salalah Port Services Co (SPS)
PO Box 105
AlHarthy Complex, PC 118
Sultanate of Oman
Tel: (+968) 567188, 567199
Fax: (+968) 567166
Website: http://www.salalahport.com

Shell Oman Marketing Company
PO Box 38
Mina Al Fahal, PC 116
Sultanate of Oman
Tel (+968) 570102
Fax: (+968) 570103
E-mail: faisal.al-hashar@smomus.simis.com

SIMPA Marketing Research & Consultancy
PO Box 208
AlHarthy Complex, PC 118
Sultanate of Oman
Tel: (+968) 701930, 701430
Fax: (+968) 701242
E-mail: simpa@omantel.net.om

Sultanate of Oman Capital Market Authority
PO Box 3359
Ruwi, PC 112
Sultanate of Oman
Tel: (+968) 771 2607
Fax: (+968) 771 7461
Website: http://www.msm.gov.om

Trowers & Hamlins
PO Box 2991
Ruwi, PC 112
Sultanate of Oman
Tel: (+968) 771 5500
Fax: (+968) 771 5544
E-mail: trowers@omantel.net.om

Val Kwaan
E-mail: kwaan@omantel.net.om

Index

References in italic indicate figures or tables.

Index of Advertisers